I0754870

HAIIM B. ROSÉN

Bio-bibliographical sketch

Haiim B. Rosén (1922-1999)

CENTRE INTERNATIONAL DE DIALECTOLOGIE GÉNÉRALE

BIOBIBLIOGRAPHIES ET EXPOSÉS

N.S. 8

HAIIM B. ROSÉN

Bio-bibliographical sketch

by Pierre SWIGGERS
followed by the late Prof. ROSÉN's text:

"The Jerusalem School of Linguistics and the Prague School"

LEUVEN
CENTRE INTERNATIONAL DE DIALECTOLOGIE GÉNÉRALE
Blijde-Inkomststraat 21

2005

A CIP record for this book is available from the Library of Congress.

ISBN 90-429-1695-8 (Peeters Leuven)
D. 2005/0602/127

FOREWORD

Haiim B. Rosén died on October 2, 1999, a few days after having finished the text of his monograph *Un demi-siècle de linguistique européenne*, to which the (hitherto unpublished) text printed here constitutes a supplement. Haiim Rosén was a careful observer, and an outstanding practitioner of European structural linguistics, which he exported to Israel and to which he conveyed a particular flavour — together with a number of colleagues (esp. Hans Jacob Polotsky) and pupils, in Jerusalem and Tel-Aviv.

Haiim's insider's knowledge, and especially his multiperspectival outlook (as a scholar trained in Europe and in Israel, as a teacher in Jerusalem, Tel-Aviv, and also a visiting professor in the United States, in Germany and, at various times, in France) made him the perfect choice for surveying, on the occasion of the *XVIe Congrès international des linguistes*, held in Paris, half a century of European linguistics (or: linguistics in Europe, with an eye to the transfer of European ideas). In fact, Haiim Rosén has witnessed almost three-quarters of a century of modern linguistics, in Europe, in the Near East and in the United States. However, the exposure to rapidly changing theories, models and fashions never turned him away from his abiding interest in structural aspects of language, in typological traits (which he consistently refused to take as "universals"), in the subtle relationships between form(s) and function(s). Haiim Rosén's linguistic career has been a constant search for establishing *la valeur* of linguistic elements, relations, and structures, always starting from what is given to us — in texts, in utterances.

Haiim Rosén's approach to language is structural(ist) in the deepest and widest sense of the term: all levels of language structure — from segmental and suprasegmental phonetics to sentential and discursive syntax — are included in the analysis, and all aspects of (oral and written) language receive due attention, the ultimate goal being the adequate understanding of how language functions in context, and how linguistic structures fulfill their expressive and communicative goals. The approach adopted is a non-dogmatic one — and explicitly stated as such —, since priority is given to language structures, not to models imposed upon language (or upon idealized structures). Admittedly, "linguistic facts" as used by a theoretical linguist — and Haiim Rosén undoubtedly was a major theoretical linguist, although he preferred to be called simply "a linguist" (interested in data and theories) — always carry a part of theory-ladenness, but one cannot deny that a philologically based approach of language structures (the approach embodied in Haiim's *opus*) is much closer to the pole of "data as such" than to the pole of "hypothetical theorizing". The philologically based approach is also less exclusive with respect to competing theories and models: it can accommodate various types of accounts and explanations, and integrate their respective merits within a polythetic ("eclectic", in the positive sense) and flexible analysis, which aims at understanding language as a typically human phenomenon.

A major contributor to linguistic structuralism, Haiim Rosén closely followed the development of linguistic science from World War II till the end of the 20th century. By descent and education he has to be assigned to structuralism in its European conception and practice, although he was also an avid reader and admirer of the writings of Sapir, Bloomfield, and their disciples. But his broad linguistic views were strongly rooted in European thought, in a neo-Humboldtian "categorial" philosophy of language and man, which was also the perspective underlying Hjelmslev's glossematics, grounded in the harmonious marriage of *humanitas* and *universitas*. "Linguistic theory is led by an inner necessity to recognize not merely the linguistic system, in its schema and its usage, in its totality and in its individuality, but also man and human society behind language, and all man's sphere of knowledge through language. At that point linguistic theory has reached its prescribed goal: *humanitas et universitas*" (Hjelmslev, *Omkring sprogteoriens grundlæggelse*, 1943; Engl. transl. 1961).

Haiim Rosén was well aware of the fact that — just as our linguistic categorizations are always approximations — classificatory labels such as "structuralism", *c.q.* "European structuralism", can be dangerously misleading, when they are taken to suggest or to imply a neatly definable "essence" or "specificity". In his monograph *Un demi-siècle de linguistique européenne*, he judiciously points out that there is "no 'European School' of linguistics; a variety of Schools exists and expands in the European scholarly space, and an autonomy of thought of mutually reconcilable Schools ensures that lines of thought and methods are not forced one upon the other" (English summary, p. 83). Drawing our attention to the existence of various forms (commonly called "schools", or "circles") of European structuralism, Haiim Rosén underscores the historical importance of the diversity of perspectives: "This pluralism eliminates dangerous inbreeding and tendencies to call forth a hegemonial position of one or the other school; a 'general tendency' or 'mainstream' seems never to have existed in Europe. The great achievements of European language science are an outcome of the interaction of ideas and tendencies during the last half-century" (p. 83-84).

The text published here — the edited version of a talk given in 1995 — presents an interesting case of interaction within the structuralist approach to language: the interaction between the Prague "School", stressing the means–ends relationship in language and combining, in a fruitful way, the synchronic and diachronic points of view, and the "École de Jérusalem", the Israel-based tradition of linguistic research (highly indebted to the writings and the teaching of Haiim Rosén and Hans Jacob Polotsky), interested in the functional analysis of language structures as observed in speech and in written texts.

*P. Swiggers**
C.I.D.G., Leuven.

* The publication of this booklet was made possible through the support of the Faculty of Humanities of the Hebrew University of Jerusalem; a special word of thanks is due to Prof. Hannah Rosén, who was instrumental in having the text of the 1995 talk fully transcribed and prepared for publication, and who provided assistance at various stages in the preparation of the brochure. A leading scholar in Latin and Celtic linguistics, Prof. Hannah Rosén is herself a prominent member and representative of the Jerusalem school of structural linguistics, whose work has received worldwide scholarly recognition (cf. L. SAWICKI – D. SHALEV eds., *Donum grammaticum. Studies in Latin and Celtic Linguistics in Honour of Hannah Rosén*, Leuven - Paris - Sterling: Peeters, 2002).

HAIIM B. ROSÉN: A BIOGRAPHICAL SKETCH

by

Pierre Swiggers

HAIIM B. ROSÉN: A BIOGRAPHICAL SKETCH*

Haiim Baruch Rosén was born as Heinz Erich Rosenrauch[1], on March 4, 1922 in Vienna. He was the son of a craftsman and a musically talented mother, who gave their child a first-class education. As a schoolboy he learned the classical languages, Greek and Latin, and also various modern European languages; in addition, he took classes in Modern Hebrew. The political climate of the 1930s and the growing anti-Semitic feelings made life in Vienna very hard for the family, and in 1938 the parents decided to leave Vienna and to emigrate to Palestine. The family arrived and settled in Palestine at the end of 1938.

In 1939-40 Haiim Rosén enrolled at the Hebrew University of Jerusalem, where he studied Classics and Hebrew. Already during his last year as a student he served in the Haganah; his military service was to span the years 1942-1949. In 1948 he participated in the foundation of the new political state of Israel (1948), and for the rest of his life he would keep a lively interest in the political and cultural life of his new homeland. In 1943 Haiim Rosén had obtained his M.A. degree, and in 1948 his Ph. D. at the Hebrew University of Jerusalem; from 1943 till 1949 he taught Latin and Hebrew grammar in high school, at the same time serving in the army.

Haiim Rosén's academic career took its start in 1949 when he was appointed at the Department of Classics at the Hebrew University of Jerusalem. His field of teaching gradually extended so as to include the comparative grammar of the Indo-European languages, (linguistic topics in) Classical Philology, and general linguistics (as applied to the description of Modern Hebrew and the Indo-European languages). In those days, general linguistics was hardly an academic subject, and it was mainly through the efforts of Haiim Rosén and his colleague, friend and

---

* *EW* I = Haiim B. Rosén, *East and West. Selected Writings*, vol. I, München, 1982; *EW* II = *East and West. Selected Writings*, vol. II, München, 1984; *EW* III = *East and West. Selected Writings*, vol. III, München, 1994.

[1] In 1949 the name was legally changed to "Haiim B. Rosén".

also mentor, Hans Jacob Polotsky that general linguistics received due recognition in Israel[2], and that the teaching of general linguistics received a place in departments where until then the (scientific and systematic) study of language had been neglected or discarded. Haiim Rosén introduced in Israel the principles and methods of European structuralism, and to a great extent also the basic ideas of American structuralism, and he was to train several generations of Classical scholars and future linguists, offering them an original synthesis of structuralist ideas — in which the intellectual debt to Prague structuralism is undoubtedly prominent — enriched with the almost unique blend of a comparative Indo-European and Semitic outlook, and the experience of a newly revived language, Ivrit. The outcome was a specific variety of "Near-Eastern" European structuralism, now commonly identified as the "Jerusalem school of linguistics", of which Haiim Rosén became the leading theoretician and practitioner[3].

The first decade of Haiim Rosén's scholarly career is marked by a strong involvement in the diffusion of the basic principles of linguistic science, and in the propagation of linguistics as a science within the academic realm. In 1954 a booklet appeared containing a series of talks on "language and history"[4], and in 1956 he published a general introduction to linguistics[5], also written in Hebrew. In his descriptive work of that period, Rosén focused on Biblical and Modern Hebrew, and published notes on topics of epigraphy and biblical philology. But he also published

---

[2] See H.B. Rosén's text "The Science of Language in Polotsky's Times" [in Hebrew], in: *'Iyunim be-'ikvot mif'alo šel Polotsky*, Jerusalem, 1988, 38-60.

[3] On the "École de Jérusalem", and for a survey of publications by the members of this school, see the text printed here, as well as Haiim Rosén's *Un demi-siècle de linguistique européenne*, Paris - Leuven, 2001, p. 19, 40 and 48 (and see p. 37 on a specific feature of the Jerusalem school: "C'est tout particulièrement dans les «petites» Écoles, comme la finlandaise et celle de Jérusalem, où l'organisation académique ne favorisait pas une séparation nette entre la philologie et la linguistique, que l'attitude décrite de contact interdisciplinaire peut fleurir et peut aussi, grâce au fait que les travaux qui y sont conduits s'appuient sur une interprétation exacte et saine des textes littéraires grâce à des analyses structurales — catégorielles et fonctionnelles — rigoureuses, apporter une contribution au progrès dans l'histoire des littératures").

[4] *Talks on Language and History* [in Hebrew], Tel-Aviv.

[5] *Introductory Topics in General Linguistics* [in Hebrew], Tel-Aviv.

articles on Indo-European, and especially on linguistic topics in ancient Greek. Alongside his linguistic descriptive work, Haiim Rosén was also involved in the (edition and) translation of classical Greek and Latin texts: he translated parts of Aristotle's *Politics* and edited Cicero's first speech against Catilina[6].

His favourite Greek author, of whom he was to become the leading specialist, was Herodotus. To Herodotus's *Historiae* he devoted, over several decades, much of his efforts, in preparing an edition of the text and a careful study of the author's language. The grammar of Herodotus's language appeared in 1962[7]; the edition of books I-IX of the *Historiae* followed much later[8]. Both works are monuments of Herodotean scholarship. The study of Herodotus was only one of Haiim Rosén's scholarly interests: others were the structural analysis of Modern Hebrew, the syntax of Biblical Hebrew and Aramaic, issues in the comparative grammar of the Indo-European languages, and — as the overarching concern — the reflection on basic problems of general linguistics (the status and nature of grammatical categories; the relationship between formal structures and functional goals; the establishing of a comprehensive framework for the study of relationships between linguistic elements, patterns, and systems, as manifested in texts).

Haiim Rosén's study of Modern Hebrew was guided by the principle of immanent systematicity; this implied a rejection of (a priori) dogmatic and puristic attitudes, and the adoption of an inductive approach, focusing on form–function relationships[9].

---

6 (with Hannah Rosén): *Aristotelis Politica III* and *Aristotelis Politica IV*, Jerusalem, 1956 and 1958. The edition *Ciceronis in Catilinam Or. I* appeared in 1958. In the 1960s Haiim Rosén collaborated with Hannah Rosén and Salomon Pines in the translation of Aristotle's *Metaphysics VII-IX* (Jerusalem, 1966).

7 *Laut- und Formenlehre der herodotischen Sprachform*, Heidelberg. A grammar of Herodotus's language, the book confronts the forms found in Herodotus with those found in the epigraphical texts. Herodotus's language is situated within a larger geographical frame of ancient Greek forms. On the importance of the undertaking, see D. Shalev, review of S. Colvin, *Dialect in Aristophanes* (1999), *Scripta Classica Israelica* 20 (2001), 275-282 (esp. 279-280).

8 *Herodotus: Historiae*, Leipzig - Stuttgart, vol. I (1987), vol. II (1997).

9 See, e.g., the two articles "Sur quelques catégories à expression adnominale en hébreu israélien", *Bulletin de la Société de Linguistique de Paris* 53:1 (1958), 316-344 [= *EW* II, 41-69] and "The Comparative Assignment of Certain Hebrew Tense Forms", in: *Proceedings of the International Conference on Semitic Studies (Jerusalem 1965)*, Jerusalem, 1969, 212-234 [= *EW* II, 229-251].

Rosén's structuralist approach of Modern Hebrew resulted in the first descriptive account of Ivrit syntax[10] and in the publication of an important textbook[11]. The most impressive outcome was the reference-work *Contemporary Hebrew*, published in 1977[12], which constitutes an original synthesis of research on all aspects of Modern Hebrew and a standard guide for further investigation.

In the late 1950s, the 1960s and 1970s Haiim Rosén also published extensively on historical topics connected with the Hebrew language; important contributions to be mentioned here are his study of the origins of the relative clauses in North-Semitic[13] and on the origin of the "accusative marker" *'t* in Biblical Hebrew[14], and his article on verbless sentences[15]. An admirable piece of philological and linguistic research is his study of the use of tenses in the Aramaic book of Daniel[16].

---

[10] *Our Hebrew, Viewed in the Light of Linguistic Methodology* [in Hebrew], Tel-Aviv; see also "Syntactical Notes on Israeli Hebrew", *Journal of the American Oriental Society* 81 (1961), 21-26 [= *EW* II, 102-107] — about determination and indetermination —; "Quelques phénomènes d'absence et de présence de l'accord dans la structure de la phrase en hébreu", *GLECS* 10 (1965), 78-84 [= *EW* II, 114-120]; "A Point of Contemporary Hebrew Syntax" [in Hebrew], in: *Shalom Sivan Memorial Volume*, Jerusalem, 1979, 141-144 [= *EW* II, 184-180; this article deals with cases of valency oversaturation].

[11] *A Textbook of Israeli Hebrew*, Chicago (later editions: 1966, 1969, 1976).

[12] *Contemporary Hebrew*, The Hague - Paris.

[13] "Zur Vorgeschichte des Relativsatzes im Nordwestsemitischen", *Archív Orientální* 27 (1959), 186-198 [= *EW* II, 309-321].

[14] "A Syntactic Feature of Early North-West Semitic: on the Prehistory of *'t*", in *Tur-Sinai Anniversary Volume*, Jerusalem, 1960, 127-142 [in Hebrew] [= *EW* II, 336-322]: in this paper, Haiim Rosén shows that the case prefix *'t* expressed the accusative function in those sentences where the absence of other constituents made it impossible to determine the relative position of the noun.

[15] "On Some Types of Verbless Sentences in Biblical Hebrew", in: *Report of the 3rd World Congress of Jewish Studies (Jerusalem 1961)*, Jerusalem, 1965, 167-173 [in Hebrew] [= *EW* II, 228-221]; in fact, this contribution contains an overall classification of Biblical Hebrew sentence types in terms of formal structure.

[16] "On the Use of the Tenses in the Aramaic of Daniel", *Journal of Semitic Studies* 6 (1961), 183-204 [= *EW* II, 285-305]: on the basis of a close examination of all verb forms in the Aramaic parts of the book of Daniel, Haiim Rosén arrives at a classification of two separata tense paradigms, for both "linear" and "point aspect" verbs: these paradigms involve the Future-volitive, the Present, the Narrative-constatative and the Subordinative.

The topics of Indo-European comparative and historical grammar dealt with by Haiim Rosén in the late 1950s, the 1960s and 1970s belong to various linguistic levels: phonological (with a prominent place given to the laryngeals, their manifestations and their reflexes)[17] and morphosyntactic[18]. It was in the early 1960s that Haiim Rosén laid the foundations of his general linguistic theory, characterized by the cross-linguistic, typological search for relationships and correlations linking forms and functions[19].

---

[17] See "Laryngalreflexe und das indogermanische 'schwache' Perfektum", *Lingua* 6 (1957), 354-373 [= *EW* I, 107-127]; "*W* als Laryngalreflex im Frühgriechischen", *Lingua* 7 (1958), 367-386 [= *EW* I, 127-146]; "Greek Evidence for Laryngeals. A Rejoinder to Prof. Cowgill", *Lingua* 10 (1961), 190-210 [= *EW* I, 147-167]; "Some Aspects of Homeric Greek Accent in Indo-European View", in: *Actes du Xe Congrès International des Linguistes (Bucarest 1967)*, Bucarest, 1970, vol. IV, 33-43 [= *EW* I, 362-372].

[18] "Die Ausdrucksform für 'veräusserlichen' und 'unveräusserlichen' Besitz im Frühgriechischen. (Das Funktionsfeld von homer. φίλος)", *Lingua* 8 (1959), 264-293 [= *EW* I, 325-354]; "Die Grammatik des Unbelegten, gezeigt an den Nominalkomposita bei Ennius", in: *Anton Reichling Volume* [= *Lingua* 21], 1968, 359-381 [= *EW* I, 231-253]; "*Vterum dolet* und Verwandtes. Zu einigen übersehenen frühlateinischen Zeugnissen impersonaler oder intransitiver Verbalkonstruktion", *Folia Linguistica* 4 (1969), 135-147 [= *EW* I, 254-266]; "Satzbau und augmentloses historisches Tempus im homerischen Tatsachenbericht", *Folia Linguistica* 6 (1973), 315-330 [= *EW* I, 373-388]; "Gedanken zur Geschichte des griechischen Satzbaus", *Die Sprache* 21 (1975), 23-36 [= *EW* I, 389-402]; "Sur quelques types de prédication en indo-européen ancien", in: *Étrennes de septantaine offertes à Michel Lejeune*, Paris, 1978, 217-222 [= *EW* I, 77-82]; "*Amamini* und die indogermanische Diathesen- und Valenzkategorien", *Zeitschrift für vergleichende Sprachforschung* 92 (1978), 143-178 [= *EW* I, 175-210].

[19] See the methodologically important article "Über einige theoretische Grundlagen der Kontrastivanalyse", *Folia Linguistica* 12 (1978), 1-16 [= *EW* I, 83-98], in which the author presents a frame for contrastive analysis of expressive (sub)systems of languages. "Eine solche, auf Systemvergleichung fußende und die Tatsache zum Ausdruck bringende Analyse, daß optimal funktionell (semantisch) gleichwertige Inhalte in den verglichenen Sprachen mit artverschiedenen sprachlichen Mitteln zum Ausdruck gebracht werden können (z.B. optimale Gleichwertigkeit einer Valenzverschiedenheit ein und desselben Lexems in Sprache A und einer lexematischen Verschiedenheit in Sprache B), hilft auch theoretische Fragen noch allgemeinerer Natur zu beleuchten, wie (1) ob Übereinstimmung der Art der Ausdrucksmittel bei Funktions-(Inhalts-)äquivalenz ein Indiz der typologischen Verwandtschaft der verglichenen Sprachen oder ein Postulat eines Universalitätsanspruchs ist, oder (2) ob die Trennung der sog. "syntaktischen" von der sog. "semantischen" Komponente in der Realisierung der sprachlichen Äußerung Anspruch auf vielsprachliche Allgemeingültigkeit zu erheben berechtigt ist" (*a.c.*, p. 3 = [*EW* I, p. 85]).

His foundational paper on a general theory of juncture, starting out from an idea formulated by Wilhelm von Humboldt (who perceived a gradation of phonemic juncture [*Verbindung*] according to the morphological status of the form segments joined, proposes an almost axiomatic system, illustrated with examples taken from Sanskrit, Greek, and Biblical Hebrew, for applying juncture (features) to various levels of analysis, ranging from the phonemic to the syntactic level[20]. In another important article, published in the *Mélanges Marcel Cohen*[21], Rosén distinguishes three non-diachronic types of successivity, and one diachronic type. As to the non-diachronic types, one of them is constituted by the successivity of levels; the other two, called "successivité analytique" (= the successive realizations of the elements of a language) and "successivité syntagmatique-sémantique" (= the successive accumulations of segments of an utterance) are recognized as the two faces of the same coin: "La progression de l'articulation des constituants immédiats correspond, *au plan du contenu*, à la progression des liaisons et niveaux *au plan de l'expression*. La successivité syntagmatique-sémantique est le signifié par rapport au signifiant qui est la succession analytique des niveaux"[22].

From the late 1970s on Haiim Rosén, while pursuing his studies of Indo-European comparative grammar and his research on Biblical and Modern Hebrew, integrates his philological work, his diachronic-comparative research and his synchronic-descriptive studies within the global, structuralist view of language he had elaborated in the previous decades, a view rooted in the Humboldtian idea that all language forms, whatever their formal diversity, have to be correlated with functional categories serving expressive and communicative goals. During the 1980s and 1990s Rosén's linguistic work is aimed at showing the applicability of the theoretical groundwork, through descriptive and historical-comparative studies on a wide variety of

---

20 "An Outline of a General Theory of Juncture", in: *Studies in Egyptology and Linguistics in Honour of H.J. Polotsky*, Jerusalem, 1964, 153-189 [= *EW* I, 19-55].

21 "Les successivités", in: *Mélanges Marcel Cohen*, The Hague - Paris, 1970, 113-129 [= *EW* I, 56-72].

22 "Les successivités", *a.c.*, p. 128 [= *EW* I, p. 71].

Indo-European and Semitic languages[23]; during this period Rosén also became more and more interested in the history of linguistics[24], of which he studied a number of key figures (Aristotle[25], Humboldt[26], Saussure[27]).

Haiim Rosén's publications during the two decades 1980-1999 span a wide variety of languages and topics: apart from the linguistic-historiographical analyses of the contribution of major figures in the history of linguistic thought, and along with his continued interest in laryngeals and their "reflexes"[28], three main fields of research can be delineated. The first is the comparative study of Indo-European syntax, a field in which Rosén's methodological observations and well-focused investigations have been of major importance[29]. The second area is that of language

---

[23] See the extensive "Part II" of *EW* III, which contains a wide variety of language-specific and comparative studies.

[24] But see already his "Some Thoughts on Aristotle's Classification of Phonemes", in: *Proceedings of the 11th International Congress of Linguists (Bologna 1972)*, Bologna, 1974, vol. I, 113-116 [= *EW* I, 73-76].

[25] "Zu Text und Interpretation der grammatischen Abschnitte in Aristoteles' Poetik und zur Umdeutung und Umformung der Redeteileinteilung bis ins orientalische Mittelalter", in: H.-J. Niederehe – K. Koerner (eds.), *History and Historiography of Linguistics. Proceedings of the IVth International Congress on the History of the Language Sciences, Trier 1987*, Amsterdam, 1990, 111-121 [= *EW* III, 74-84]; "Aristotle's Thoughts on Language – An Outgrowth of an 'Intellectual Climate'", in: J. De Clercq – P. Desmet (eds.), *Florilegium Historiographiae Linguisticae*, Leuven, 1994, 87-96.

[26] "Wilhelm von Humboldts Begriff des Phonems", in: *Energeia und Ergon. Festschrift Eugenio Coseriu*, Tübingen, 1988, vol. II, 11-17 [= *EW* III, 30-36]; "Wilhelm von Humboldt – Philosopher or the First Structural Linguist?", *Bulletin of the Language Institute of Gakushuín University* 12 (1989), 3-39 [= *EW* III, 37-73]. The latter text, which stresses the intrinsic importance of philology for language science in Humboldt's view, contains an addendum concerning the relationship between Humboldt and Saussure.

[27] "Les lois synchroniques et les lois diachroniques dans le *Cours* de Saussure", *Cahiers Ferdinand de Saussure* 40 (1986), 91-103 [= *EW* III, 17-29].

[28] See "Laryngales, allomorphes et la validité de quelques 'lois phonétiques'", in: *Athlon. Satura grammatica in honorem Francisci R. Adrados*, Madrid, 1984, vol. I, 431-442 [= *EW* III, 149-160]; "On the Nature and Essence of Laryngeal Reflexes With Glimpses on the Emergence of a Terminological Usage", *Historische Sprachforschung* 112 (1999), 175-187. The latter article contains a short survey of the history of the term "reflex" as used by Indo-Europeanists.

[29] Apart from the very important monograph *Is a Comparative Indo-European Syntax Possible?*, Innsbruck, 1994, see the articles: "Some More Noteworthy

history, more specifically of the languages spoken in Canaan — from Pre-Canaanite to Classical Hebrew and, after a long period of discontinuity, Modern Hebrew. A defining characteristic of Rosén's approach to language history is the constant preoccupation with investigating the history of languages in their multiple contacts, and in their broader cultural and linguistic setting[30]. The third field, more diversified as to the language materials studied, is the one which best exemplifies Haiim Rosén's conception of general linguistics and the way in which he conceived his contribution to the Jerusalem school of linguistics (and to the field of linguistics). Here we deal with research, in which philology and linguistics fully harmonize[31],

Features of 'Primitive' Indo-European Syntax", *Journal of Indo-European Studies* 15 (1987), 62-75 [= *EW* III, 174-187]; "On Some Types of So-Called 'Impersonality' and Verbal Valency in Indo-European", in: R. Beekes *et al.* (eds.), *Rekonstruktion und relative Chronologie. Akten der VIII. Fachtagung der Indogermanischen Gesellschaft, Leiden 1987*, Leiden, 1992, 383-390 [= *EW* III, 188-195]; "Does a Comparative Indo-European Syntax Become Possible?" [in Russian], *Voprosy Jazykoznanija* 1993/1, 5-21.

[30] See the following articles and books: *L'hébreu et ses rapports avec le monde classique. Essai d'évaluation culturelle*, Paris, 1979; "La pluralité des langues devant la conscience religieuse juive", in: *IIIe et IVe Colloques d'histoire des religions, organisés par la Société Ernest Renan*, Paris, 1979, 89-94; "Die Sprachsituation im römischen Palästina", in: G. Neumann – J. Untermann (eds.), *Die Sprachen im römischen Reich der Kaiserzeit*, Köln - Bonn, 1980, 215-239 [= *EW* I, 489-513]; *La nature de l'hébreu médiéval. Une grande langue de tradition à différenciation régionale*, Tel-Aviv, 1986; "Second Thoughts on Semitisms in the Septuagint and the 'Tongue in which the Torah spoke'" [in Hebrew], in: *Proceedings of the 5th Annual Meeting, Societatis Linguisticae Europaeae Sodalicium Israëlense*, 1988, 26-31; "**Ekwos* et l'«hippologie» canaanéenne — Réflexions étymologiques", in: L. Isebaert (ed.), *Studia etymologica indoeuropaea memoriae A.J. Van Windekens dicata*, Leuven, 1991, 233-237 [= *EW* III, 437-441]; "Language Survival, Revival, and Typology — The Case of Hebrew", in: *Actes du XVe Congrès des Linguistes, Québec 1992*, Québec, 1993, vol. IV, 197-200; *Hebrew at the Crossroads of Cultures. From Outgoing Antiquity to the Middle Ages*, Leuven - Paris, 1995; "The Lexical Semitisms of Septuagint Greek as a Reflex of the History of the Hebrew Vocabulary — Implications Concerning Lexical Diachrony and Historical Lexicography", in: *Historical, Indo-European, and Lexicographical Studies. A Festschrift for Ladislav Zgusta on the Occasion of his 70th Birthday*, Berlin - New York, 1997, 301-318; "Pre-Canaanite: A People, a Language, and a Culture", *Minos* 31/32 (1997), 433-446.

[31] The fruitful combination of both is also manifest in Haiim Rosén's metrical-stylistical studies; see e.g., "Nouveaux regards sur l'expression poétique

focusing on general issues of form-function correlations, across linguistic families and language stages, always in strict obedience to the basic principles of structuralism. The topics dealt with by Haiim Rosén, on a number of occasions in joint publications with Hannah Rosén[32], are among the most basic ones of linguistic description and theorizing: nominal categories[33], the marking of possession-relationships (in connection with case syntax)[34], the formal devices used in *énonciation*[35], the structure and function of periphrastic expressions[36], and — most impor-

d'Homère", *Revue des Études grecques* 102 (1989), 263-283 [= *EW* III, 259-279]; "La structure de l'énoncé poétique d'Homère — Rythme tonique et rythme syntaxique", *LALIES. Actes des sessions de linguistique et de littérature* 10 (1992), 329-343 [= *EW* III, 286-300]; "La conception de la diction épique dans l'esprit des poètes républicains et leurs successeurs", in: Cl. Moussy *et al.* (eds.), *De lingua Latina novae quaestiones. Actes du Xᵉ Colloque International de Linguistique latine, Paris-Sèvres, 19-23 avril 1999*, Leuven - Paris - Sterling, 2001, 981-993.

[32] Most prominently: *On Moods and Tenses of the Latin Verb. Two Essays Dedicated to H.J. Polotsky on the Occasion of his 75th Birthday*, München, 1980.

[33] "Über einige wenig berücksichtigte morphologische Gesichtspunkte zur Frage der Entstehung der nominalen Genuskategorien im Indogermanischen", in: B. Schlerath – V. Bittner (eds.), *Grammatische Kategorien: Funktion und Geschichte. Akten der VII. Fachtagung der Indogermanischen Gesellschaft, Berlin 1983*, Wiesbaden, 1985, 411-423 [= *EW* III, 161-173]; "On Some Nominal Morphological Categories in Biblical Hebrew", in: *On the Dignity of Man. Oriental and Classical studies in honour of Frithiof Rundgren*, Stockholm, 1986, 355-365 [= *EW* III, 418-428]; "*Ius*, *fas* et l'attribution du genre grammatical aux abstraits latins à suffixe comportant *-s*", in: M. Lavency – D. Longrée (eds.), *Actes du Vᵉ Colloque de Linguistique latine, Louvain-la-Neuve - Borzée*, Louvain-la-Neuve, 1989, 379-390 [= *EW* III, 309-320]; "Remarques à propos du genre grammatical en hébreu biblique", in: J. Lentin – A. Lonnet (eds.), *Mélanges David Cohen. Études sur le langage, les langues, les dialectes, les littératures offertes par ses élèves, ses collègues, ses amis [...] à l'occasion de son quatre-vingtième anniversaire*, Paris, 2003, 581-594.

[34] "A Marginal Note on Sanskrit Case-Syntax", in: Subhadra Kumar Sen (ed.), *Hanjamana*, Calcutta, 1989, 33-39 [= *EW* III, 199-205; concerning the possessive dative]; "'Having' in Petronius", in: G. Tournoy – Th. Sacré (eds.), *Pegasus Devocatus. Studia in honorem C. Arri Nuri sive Harry C. Schnur*, Leuven, 1992, 101-117 [= *EW* III, 332-348].

[35] See: "Rhème et non-rhème: entités de langue. Pour une typologie des moyens d'expression formels", *Bulletin de la Société de Linguistique de Paris* 82:1 (1987), 135-162 [= *EW* III, 113-140]; "Constituants pluricomponentiels et caractérisation de la fonction énonciative", in: *La phrase – Énonciation et information* (*Mémoires de la Société de Linguistique de Paris*, n.s. 2), 1994, 57-73.

[36] See especially *Die Periphrase: Wesen und Entstehung*, Innsbruck, 1992, and "Weiteres über die Entstehung der periphrastischen 'Perfekt'-Formen im

tantly — the classification of sentence types and the determination of criteria for sentence analysis[37].

Haiim B. Rosén's merits as a scholar, as a teacher and spokesman of linguistics, and his human qualities have received universal recognition. His colleagues, friends and students honoured him with a three-volume selection of his writings, which appeared between 1982 and 1994[38]. He was a member of various linguistic societies and associations: the Linguistic Society of America, the Societas Linguistica Europaea (of which he was the vice president in 1978), the Société de Linguistique de Paris, the Linguistic Circle of New York, the Société Asiatique, the Indogermanische Gesellschaft, the Société des études grecques and the Groupe d'études linguistiques chamito-sémitiques (*GLECS*). In Israel, he was elected to the National Academy of Sciences and Humanities in 1981. He was, since 1967, the representative of Israel in the Comité international permanent des linguistes (*CIPL*), and played an important role in the organization of the XVIth Congress of Linguists in Paris, in

Lateinischen. Zum Begriff 'Zustand des Akt-(Resultats)besitzes'", in: *Wege zur Universalienforschung. Sprachwissenschaftliche Beiträge zum 60. Geburtstag von Hansjakob Seiler*, Tübingen, 1980, 311-316 [= *EW* III, 303-308].

[37] See, apart from the studies already referred to concerning rhematicity and *énonciation* (cf. note 35), the following articles: "Aspects of the Study of the Order of the Sentence Parts in Israeli Hebrew" [in Hebrew], in: *Proceedings of the VIIIth World Congress of Jewish Studies*, 1983, section IV, 43-49 [= *EW* III, 460-453; a study of the constituent order in Israeli Hebrew prose]; "Funktionelle Parameter der neuhochdeutschen Satzstellung", in: *Studia Linguistica, Diachronica et Synchronica Werner Winter sexagenario dedicata*, Berlin, 1985, 735-749 [= *EW* III, 385-399]; "*Quam quisque norit artem, in hac se exerceat* and the Typology of Relative Clauses", in: B. García-Hernández (ed.), *Estudios de Lingüística latina. Actas del IX Coloquio Internacional de Lingüística latina, Madrid 1997*, Madrid, 1998, 713-729 [in this study Haiim Rosén shows that the type *quam quisque* constitutes a sequence of two relatives which form a type of relative clauses common in a number of ancient Indo-European languages; only in Imperial Latin did *quisque* gain an autonomous status as an indefinite pronoun]; "Der Wirkungsbereich des Wackernagelschen Gesetzes und die Entstehung der Präpositionen", in: P. Anreiter *et al.* (eds.), *Studia Celtica et Indogermanica. Festschrift für Wolfgang Meid zum 70. Geburtstag*, Budapest, 1999, 385-396.

[38] *East and West. Selected Writings in Linguistics*, vol. 1 (1982), vol. 2 (1984), vol. 3 (1994).

1997[39]. His international scientific recognition appears from the many visiting professorships he held: in 1958-1959 at the University of Chicago, in 1990 at the Universität Tübingen, and on several occasions in Paris (1965-1966 at the Sorbonne, 1972, 1978 and 1985 at the École Pratique des Hautes Études, and in 1975 at the Collège de France[40]). Among the important awards he received during his lifetime, mention should be made of the Israel State Prize in the Humanities, which he received in 1978, and the Alexander von Humboldt Research Award, which was bestowed on him in 1992.

[39] Cf. J. Perrot in *Un demi-siècle...* [*o.c.*, n. 3], p. 7: "Représentant d'Israël à l'Assemblée Générale du Comité International Permanent des Linguistes, il y faisait volontiers entendre sa voix pour présenter des propositions en vue d'une participation plus effective de la communauté internationale des linguistes aux affaires relevant de la compétence du CIPL. Quand le moment est venu d'organiser le XVIe Congrès des linguistes, il a plaidé efficacement en faveur du choix de Paris, qui lui tenait à cœur. Heureux d'avoir ainsi contribué à la décision qui a permis à la France d'accueillir des linguistes du monde entier près d'un demi-siècle après le premier Congrès de Paris, organisé en 1948 sous la présidence de Joseph Vendryes, Haiim Rosén, invité à présenter un rapport sur le développement de la linguistique en Europe depuis le milieu du XXe siècle, a voulu faire plus que cette simple contribution à une séance plénière, et il a tenté de cerner à cette occasion, dans une large approche, les traits les plus caractéristiques de l'esprit et des orientations théoriques et méthodologiques des linguistes européens au cours du dernier demi-siècle, ainsi que leur apport au développement des connaissances sur les structures et l'histoire des langues".

[40] The seminar given at the Collège de France was published in 1979 as a book under the title *L'hébreu et ses rapports avec le monde classique*.

SELECTIVE LIST OF PUBLICATIONS BY HAIIM B. ROSÉN*

1948

– "Sur quelques bases nominales à préfixe *m-* en hébreu biblique". *Revue biblique* 55. 72-80.

1950-1

– "The Influence of Hebrew in Other Languages, I-II" [in Hebrew]. *Lešonénu La'am* 12. 21-24; 13. 17-22.
– "Ways and Means in Linguistic Investigation" [in Hebrew]. *Lešonénu La'am* 14. 8-12; 15. 6-11; 17. 114.

1951

– "Note on Byblos". *Vetus Testamentum* 1. 306.
– "A Practice of Early Canaanite Writing" [in Hebrew]. *Lešonénu* 17. 226-230.

1952

– "Remarques descriptives sur le parler hébreu-israélien moderne". *GLECS* 6. 4-7.

1953

– "Remarques au sujet de la phonologie de l'hébreu biblique". *Revue biblique* 60. 30-40.

1954

– ***Talks on Language and History*** [in Hebrew]. Tel Aviv: Chechik.
– "The Stele of Lemnos, its Text and Alphabetic System". *Scripta Hierosolymitana* 1. 1-20.

* For a full bibliography up to 1994, see H.B. ROSÉN, *East and West. Selected Writings in Linguistics*, vol. I and vol. III; a bibliography of H.B. Rosén's publications between 1980 and 2000 can be found in a commemorative fascicle published (2001) by the Israel Academy of Sciences and Humanities.

1955

– ***Our Hebrew, Viewed in the Light of Linguistic Methodology*** [in Hebrew]. Tel Aviv: Am-Oved.
– "*Arawna* — nom hittite?". *Vetus Testamentum* 5. 318-320.

1956

– (with Hannah Rosén) ***Aristotelis Politica III, in Hebraicum sermonem uerterunt breuique adnotatione indicibusque instruxerunt*** [...]. Jerusalem: Politeia.
– ***Introductory Topics in General Linguistics*** [in Hebrew]. Tel Aviv: Lamanxil.
– "The Components of Linguistic Science" [in Hebrew]. *Lešonénu La'am* 66. 17-20.
– "Aspects and Tenses in Biblical Hebrew" [in Hebrew]. In: *Biram Anniversary Volume*, 205-218. Jerusalem: Kiryat-Séfer.
– "The *mfu'al* Nominal Base in Israeli Hebrew" [in Hebrew]. *Lešonénu* 20. 139-148.

1957

– "Laryngalreflexe und das indogermanische 'schwache' Perfektum". *Lingua* 6. 354-373.
– "Die 'zweiten' Tempora des Griechischen: Zum Prädikatsausdruck beim griechischen Verbum". *Museum Helveticum* 14. 133-154.
– "Notes on Some Early Latin Inscriptions". *Mnemosyne* 4: 10. 239-246. [corr. *Mnemosyne* 4: 11. 156].

1958

– (with Hannah Rosén) ***Aristotelis Politica IV, in Hebraicum sermonem uerterunt breuique adnotatione indicibusque instruxerunt*** [...]. Jerusalem: Politeia.
– ***Good Hebrew: Studies in the Syntax of 'Correct' Language*** [in Hebrew]. Jerusalem: Kiryat-Séfer. [1967²; 1977³]
– ***Ciceronis in Catilinam Or. I adiectis epistulis aliquot*** [in Hebrew]. Tel-Aviv: Omanuth.
– "*W* als Laryngalreflex im Frühgriechischen". *Lingua* 7. 367-386.
– "Sur quelques catégories à expression adnominale en hébreu israélien". *Bulletin de la Société de Linguistique de Paris* 53:1. 316-344.

– “L’hébreu-israélien”. *Revue des études juives* 117. 59-90.
– “La lingua hebraico-israeliana”. *Il Ponte* 14:12. 1568-1581.

1959

– “Die Ausdrucksform für ‘veräusserlichen’ und ‘unveräusserlichen’ Besitz im Frühgriechischen. (Das Funktionsfeld von homer. φίλος)”. *Lingua* 8. 264-293.
– “Zur Vorgeschichte des Relativsatzes im Nordwestsemitischen”. *Archív Orientální* 27. 186-198.

1960

– (with I. MEHLMAN and Y. SHAKED, eds.) ***A Foundation Word List of Hebrew*** [in Hebrew and English]. Jerusalem: Department for Education and Culture in the Diaspora.
– “A Syntactic Feature of Early North-West Semitic: on the Prehistory of *’t*”. In: *Tur-Sinai Anniversary Volume*, 127-142 [in Hebrew]. Jerusalem: Kiryat-Séfer.

1961

– “Greek Evidence for Laryngeals. A Rejoinder to Prof. Cowgill”. *Lingua* 10. 190-210.
– “Arrius’ Speech Again”. *Mnemosyne* 14:3. 224-232.
– “Syntactical Notes on Israeli Hebrew”. *Journal of the American Oriental Society* 81. 21-26.
– “On the Use of the Tenses in the Aramaic of Daniel”. *Journal of Semitic Studies* 6. 183-204.

1962

– ***Eine Laut- und Formenlehre der herodotischen Sprachform***. Heidelberg: Winter.
– ***Elementa Linguae Latinae***. Tel-Aviv: Omanuth. [2 vols]
– ***A Textbook of Israeli Hebrew***. Chicago: The University of Chicago Press. [1966^2; 1969^3; 1976^4]
– “The ‘Mycenaean’ Documents — the Present State of Our Knowledge” [in Hebrew]. *Eškolot* 4. 1-56.

1963

– “Palestinian κοινή in Rabbinic Illustration”. *Journal of Semitic Studies* 8. 56-72.

1964

– "An Outline of a General Theory of Juncture". In: *Studies in Egyptology and Linguistics in Honour of H.J. Polotsky*, 153-189. Jerusalem: The Israel Exploration Society.
– "Some Possible Systemic Changes in a Semitic System of Language". In: *Proceedings of the 9th International Congress of Linguists (Cambridge, Mass. 1962)*, 904-909. London - The Hague - Paris: Mouton.

1965

– "Quelques phénomènes d'absence et de présence de l'accord dans la structure de la phrase en hébreu". *GLECS* 10. 78-84.
– "On Some Types of Verbless Sentences in Biblical Hebrew" [in Hebrew]. In: *Report of the 3rd World Congress of Jewish Studies (Jerusalem 1961)*, 167-173. Jerusalem: World Union of Jewish Studies.

1966

– (with Hannah Rosén and Salomon Pines) ***Aristotelis Metaphysica VII-IX, in Hebraicum sermonem uerterunt breuique adnotatione indicibusque instruxerunt*** [...]. Jerusalem: Magnes Press.
– "Composition adjectivale et adjectifs composés en hébreu-israélien". *GLECS* 10. 126-135.

1967

– "On the Recommended 'Classroom Pronunciation' for Teaching Classical Greek in Israel" [in Hebrew]. In: *'Doron'. B. Katz Jubilee Volume*, 45-58. Tel-Aviv: Tel-Aviv University Student Union Publ. House.

1968

– ***Strukturalgrammatische Beiträge zum Verständnis Homers***. Amsterdam: North-Holland Publ. Company. [1985^2; München: Fink]
– "Die Grammatik des Unbelegten, gezeigt an den Nominalkomposita bei Ennius". In: *Anton Reichling Volume* [= *Lingua* 21]. 359-381.

1969

– "*Vterum dolet* und Verwandtes. Zu einigen übersehenen frühlateinischen Zeugnissen impersonaler oder intransitiver Verbalkonstruktion". *Folia Linguistica* 4. 135-147.

– “The Comparative Assignment of Certain Hebrew Tense Forms”. In: *Proceedings of the International Conference on Semitic Studies (Jerusalem 1965)*, 212-234. Jerusalem: The Israel Academy of Sciences and Humanities.
– “Israel Language Policy, Language Teaching and Linguistics”. *Ariel* 25. 92-123.

1970

– “Some Aspects of Homeric Greek Accent in Indo-European View”. In: *Actes du Xe Congrès International des Linguistes (Bucarest 1967)*, vol. IV, 33-43. Bucarest: Éditions de l’Académie de la République socialiste de Roumanie.
– “Les successivités”. In: *Mélanges Marcel Cohen*, 113-129. The Hague - Paris: Mouton.
– “Retrouver la Bible à travers l’hébreu de nos jours”. *Revue d’Histoire et de Philosophie Religieuses* 2. 109-126.

1972

– “Motifs and τόποι from the New Comedy in the New Testament”. *Ancient Society* 3. 245-257.

1973

– “Satzbau und augmentloses historisches Tempus im homerischen Tatsachenbericht”. *Folia Linguistica* 6. 315-330.

1974

– “Some Thoughts on Aristotle’s Classification of Phonemes”. In: *Proceedings of the 11th International Congress of Linguists (Bologna 1972)*, vol. I, 113-116. Bologna: Il Mulino.
– “La position descriptive et comparative des formes contextuelles en hébreu”. In: *Actes du Ier Congrès international de linguistique sémitique et chamito-sémitique (Paris 1969)*, 244-253. The Hague - Paris: Mouton.

1975

– “Gedanken zur Geschichte des griechischen Satzbaus”. *Die Sprache* 21. 23-36.
– “אנכי et אני: essai de grammaire, interprétation et traduction”. In: *Mélanges André Neher*, 253-272. Paris: Adrien-Maisonneuve.

1976

– “Ein Überrest eines silbenschnittbezeichnenden byzantinischen Akzentuierungssystems”. *Helikon* 15/16. 372-389.

1977

– ***Contemporary Hebrew.*** The Hague - Paris: Mouton.

1978

– “Sur quelques types de prédication en indo-européen ancien”. In: *Étrennes de septantaine offertes à Michel Lejeune*, 217-222. Paris: Klincksieck.
– “*Amamini* und die indogermanische Diathesen- und Valenzkategorien”. *Zeitschrift für vergleichende Sprachforschung* 92. 143-178.
– “Über einige theoretische Grundlagen der Kontrastivanalyse”. *Folia Linguistica* 12. 1-16.
– “Reflexes of Extinct Phonemes in Semitic”. *Bulletin of the School of Oriental and African Studies* 41. 443-452.

1979

– ***L’hébreu et ses rapports avec le monde classique. Essai d’évaluation culturelle.*** Paris: Geuthner.
– “*Septentrio* und Verwandtes”. *Zeitschrift für vergleichende Sprachforschung* 93. 90-99.
– “A Point of Contemporary Hebrew Syntax” [in Hebrew]. In: *Shalom Sivan Memorial Volume*, 141-144. Jerusalem: Kiryat-Séfer.
– “La pluralité des langues devant la conscience religieuse juive”. In: *IIIe et IVe Colloques d’histoire des religions, organisés par la Société Ernest Renan*, 89-94. Orsay: Centre interdisciplinaire d’Étude de l’Évolution des Idées, des Sciences et des Techniques.

1980

– (with Hannah ROSÉN) ***On Moods and Tenses of the Latin Verb. Two Essays Dedicated to H.J. Polotsky on the Occasion of his 75th Birthday.*** München: Fink.
– “Die Sprachsituation im römischen Palästina”. In: G. NEUMANN – J. UNTERMANN (eds.), *Die Sprachen im römischen Reich der Kaiserzeit*, 215-239. Köln - Bonn: Rheinland Verlag.
– “Weiteres über die Entstehung der periphrastischen ‘Perfekt’-Formen im Lateinischen. Zum Begriff ‘Zustand des Akt-(Resultats)-

besitzes'". In: *Wege zur Universalienforschung. Sprachwissenschaftliche Beiträge zum 60. Geburtstag von Hansjakob Seiler*, 311-316. Tübingen: Narr.

1982

– ***East and West. Selected Writings in Linguistics.*** Part I: ***General and Indo-European Linguistics.*** München: Fink.
– "Questions d'interprétation de textes juridiques grecs de la plus ancienne époque — La contribution de la philologie à la compréhension juridique". In: *Symposion 1977* (*Akten der Gesellschaft für griechische und hellenistische Rechtsgeschichte*, 3), 9-32.

1983

– "Diachronic Syntax and the Revival of Hebrew". In: *Proceedings of the XIIIth International Congress of Linguists, Tokyo 1982*, 743-747. Tokyo: Gakushuín University.
– "Aspects of the Study of the Order of the Sentence Parts in Israeli Hebrew" [in Hebrew]. In: *Proceedings of the VIIIth World Congress of Jewish Studies*, section IV, 43-49.
– "Was Herodotus Aware of Rhetoric? On the usefulness of linguistic analyses for a deepening of our understanding of historiography" [in Hebrew]. In: *Sefer Yiṣḥaq 'Aryeh Seeligmann (Isac Leo Seeligmann Memorial Volume)*, vol. II, 499-508. Jerusalem: Rubinstein.

1984

– "Zu Grundfragen der gotischen Lexikographie — Zwei Wortfeldstudien". In: *Linguistica et Philologica: Gedenkschrift für Björn Collinder*, 369-390. Wien: Braumüller.
– "Laryngales, allomorphes et la validité de quelques 'lois phonétiques'". In: *Athlon. Satura grammatica in honorem Francisci R. Adrados*, vol. I, 431-442. Madrid: Gredos.

1985

– ***East and West. Selected Writings in Linguistics.*** Part II: ***Hebrew and Semitic Linguistics.*** München: Fink.
– "Funktionelle Parameter der neuhochdeutschen Satzstellung". In: *Studia Linguistica, Diachronica et Synchronica Werner Winter sexagenario dedicata*, 735-749. Berlin: de Gruyter.

– "Über einige wenig berücksichtigte morphologische Gesichtspunkte zur Frage der Entstehung der nominalen Genuskategorien im Indogermanischen". In: B. SCHLERATH – V. BITTNER (eds.), *Grammatische Kategorien: Funktion und Geschichte. Akten der VII. Fachtagung der Indogermanischen Gesellschaft, Berlin 1983*, 411-423. Wiesbaden: Harrassowitz.

1986

– ***La nature de l'hébreu médiéval. Une grande langue de tradition à différenciation régionale.*** Tel-Aviv: Chaim Rosenberg School of Jewish Studies.
– "Les lois synchroniques et les lois diachroniques dans le *Cours* de Saussure". *Cahiers Ferdinand de Saussure* 40. 91-103.
– " Ἄνθρωπος". *Zeitschrift für vergleichende Sprachforschung* 99. 243-244.
– "On Some Nominal Morphological Categories in Biblical Hebrew". In: *On the Dignity of Man. Oriental and Classical Studies in Honour of Frithiof Rundgren*, 355-365. Stockholm: Almqvist & Wiksell.

1987

– ***Herodotus, Historiae.*** Vol. I, libros I-IV continens. Leipzig: Teubner.
– "Rhème et non-rhème: entités de langue. Pour une typologie des moyens d'expression formels". *Bulletin de la Société de Linguistique de Paris* 82:1. 135-162.
– "Some More Noteworthy Features of 'Primitive' Indo-European Syntax". *Journal of Indo-European Studies* 15. 62-75.
– "On 'Normal' Full Root Structure and its Historical Development". In: A. GIACALONE RAMAT *et al.* (eds.), *Papers from the 7th International Conference on Historical Linguistics, Pavia 1985*, 535-544. Amsterdam: Benjamins.

1988

– ***Early Greek Grammar and Thought in Heraclitus. The Emergence of the Article.*** Jerusalem: Israel Academy of Sciences and Humanities.
– "The Science of Language in Polotsky's Times" [in Hebrew]. In: *'Iyunim be-'ikvot mif'alo šel Polotsky*, 38-60. Jerusalem: Israel Academy of Sciences and Humanities.

– "Der griechische 'Dativus Absolutus' und indogermanische 'unpersönliche' Partizipialkonstruktionen". *Zeitschrift für vergleichende Sprachforschung* 101. 92-103.
– "Wilhelm von Humboldts Begriff des Phonems". In: *Energeia und Ergon. Festschrift Eugenio Coseriu*, vol. II, 11-17. Tübingen: Narr.
– "Second Thoughts on Semitisms in the Septuagint and the 'Tongue in which the Torah spoke'" [in Hebrew]. In: *Proceedings of the 5th Annual Meeting, Societatis Linguisticae Europaeae Sodalicium Israëlense*, 26-31.

1989

– "Nouveaux regards sur l'expression poétique d'Homère". *Revue des Études grecques* 102. 263-283.
– "Wilhelm von Humboldt — Philosopher or the First Structural Linguist?". *Bulletin of the Language Institute of Gakushuín University* 12. 3-39.
– "*Ius, fas* et l'attribution du genre grammatical aux abstraits latins à suffixe comportant *-s*". In: M. LAVENCY – D. LONGRÉE (eds.), *Actes du Ve Colloque de Linguistique latine, Louvain-la-Neuve – Borzée*, 379-390. Louvain-la-Neuve: Peeters.
– "A Marginal Note on Sanskrit Case-Syntax". In: S. KUMAR SEN (ed.), *Hanjamana*, 33-39. Calcutta: University of Calcutta Press.

1990

– "Zu Text und Interpretation der grammatischen Abschnitte in Aristoteles' Poetik und zur Umdeutung und Umformung der Redeteileinteilung bis ins orientalische Mittelalter". In: H.-J. NIEDEREHE – K. KOERNER (eds.), *History and Historiography of Linguistics. Proceedings of the IVth International Congress on the History of the Language Sciences, Trier 1987*, 111-121. Amsterdam: Benjamins.

1991

– "Probable Substratum Features in the Expansion of Republican Latin". In: R. COLEMAN (ed.), *New Studies in Latin Linguistics. Selected Papers from the 4th International Colloquium on Latin Linguistics, Cambridge 1987*, 23-33. Amsterdam: Benjamins.
– "Eine andere Antwort auf die Ahhiyawa-Frage". *Indogermanische Forschungen* 96. 46-51.

– "**Ekwos* et l'«hippologie» canaanéenne — Réflexions étymologiques". In: L. ISEBAERT (ed.), *Studia etymologica indoeuropaea memoriae A.J. Van Windekens dicata*, 233-237. Leuven: Peeters.
– "Some Thoughts on the System of Designation of the Cardinal Points in Ancient Semitic Languages". In: *Semitic Studies in Honor of Wolf Leslau on the Occasion of his Eighty-Fifth Birthday*, vol. II, 1337-1344. Wiesbaden: Harrassowitz.

1992

– ***Die Periphrase: Wesen und Entstehung***. Innsbruck: Innsbrucker Beiträge zur Sprachwissenschaft.
– "'Having' in Petronius". In: G. TOURNOY – Th. SACRÉ (eds.), *Pegasus Devocatus. Studia in honorem C. Arri Nuri sive Harry C. Schnur*, 101-117. Leuven: Leuven University Press.
– "La structure de l'énoncé poétique d'Homère — Rythme tonique et rythme syntaxique". *LALIES. Actes des sessions de linguistique et de littérature* 10. 329-343.
– "Die Komposita mit *co(n)-* in funktioneller und vergleichender Sicht". In: O. PANAGL – Th. KRISCH (eds.), *Latein und Indogermanisch. Akten des Kolloquiums der Indogermanischen Gesellschaft, Salzburg 1986*, 357-367. Innsbruck: Innsbrucker Beiträge zur Sprachwissenschaft.
– "On Some Types of So-Called 'Impersonality' and Verbal Valency in Indo-European". In: R. BEEKES *et al.* (eds.), *Rekonstruktion und relative Chronologie. Akten der VIII. Fachtagung der Indogermanischen Gesellschaft, Leiden 1987*, 383-390. Innsbruck: Innsbrucker Beiträge zur Sprachwissenschaft.

1993

– "Does a Comparative Indo-European Syntax Become Possible?" [in Russian]. *Voprosy Jazykoznanija* 1993/1. 5-21.
– "Notes on the Grammar of the Biblical Hebrew Verb" [in Hebrew]. In: *Xikre 'ever va-'arav (Joshua Blau Jubilee Volume)*, 507-513. Tel-Aviv - Jerusalem.
– "Ἱστορίης ἀπόδεξις — Ein Problem der herodotischen Textkritik". *Glotta* 71. 146-153.
– "Language Survival, Revival, and Typology — The Case of Hebrew". In: *Actes du XVe Congrès des Linguistes, Québec 1992*, vol. IV, 197-200. Québec: Presses de l'Université Laval.

1994

– ***East and West III. Selected Writings in Linguistics.*** Part III. München: Fink.
– ***Is a Comparative Indo-European Syntax Possible?*** Innsbruck: Innsbrucker Beiträge zur Sprachwissenschaft.
– "Constituants pluricomponentiels et caractérisation de la fonction énonciative". In: *La phrase — Énonciation et information* (*Mémoires de la Société de Linguistique de Paris*, n.s. 2), 57-73.
– "À propos de quelques rapports entre la grammaire indienne et la grammaire arabe". In: G. Jucquois – P. Swiggers – Chr. Vielle (eds.), *Comparatisme, Mythologie, Langages. En hommage à Claude Lévi-Strauss*, 331-346. Leuven: Peeters.
– "Aristotle's Thoughts on Language — An Outgrowth of an 'Intellectual Climate'". In: J. De Clercq – P. Desmet (eds.), *Florilegium Historiographiae Linguisticae*, 87-96. Leuven: Peeters.

1995

– ***Hebrew at the Crossroads of Cultures. From Outgoing Antiquity to the Middle Ages.*** Leuven - Paris: Peeters.
– "Wiederum *ignominia*". In: W. Smoczyński (ed.), *Analecta Indoeuropaea Cracoviensia Ioannis Safarewicz memoriae dicata*, 349-353. Kraków: Universitas Cracoviae.

1996

– "Zur Erschliessung der Quellen und der Lautwerte des gotischen Alphabets". In: W. Smoczyński (ed.), *Kuryłowicz Memorial Volume*, I, 469-481. Kraków: Universitas Cracoviae.
– "Lat. *rete*". *Indogermanische Forschungen* 100. 210-212.
– "*Pons*, *mons*, *fons*, *dens* and the Indo-European Stock of the Latin Lexical Heritage". In: H. Rosén (ed.), *Aspects of Latin. Papers from the Seventh International Colloquium on Latin Linguistics, Jerusalem 1993*, 127-133. Innsbruck: Innsbrucker Beiträge zur Sprachwissenschaft.
– "Phonological Principles in Transfer of Alphabets" [in Hebrew]. In: *Proceedings of the 11th and 12th Annual Meetings of the Societatis Linguisticae Europaeae Sodalicium Israëlense*, 31-40.

1997

– ***Herodotus, Historiae.*** Vol. II, libros V-IX continens. Stuttgart - Leipzig: Teubner.

– "The Lexical Semitisms of Septuagint Greek as a Reflex of the History of the Hebrew Vocabulary — Implications Concerning Lexical Diachrony and Historical Lexicography". In: *Historical, Indo-European, and Lexicographical Studies. A Festschrift for Ladislav Zgusta on the Occasion of his 70th Birthday*, 301-318. Berlin - New York: Mouton de Gruyter.
– "On Human Society and Culture, Intellect and Language Structure — As mirrored by structuralism in both its facets" [in Hebrew]. In: *Proceedings of the Israel Academy of Sciences and Humanities* 8 (5). 85-108.
– "Pre-Canaanite: A People, a Language, and a Culture". *Minos* 31/32. 433-446.

1998

– "*Quam quisque norit artem, in hac se exerceat* and the Typology of Relative Clauses". In: B. GARCÍA-HERNÁNDEZ (ed.), *Estudios de Lingüística latina. Actas del IX Coloquio Internacional de Lingüística latina, Madrid 1997*, 713-729. Madrid: Gredos.
– "La linguistique en Europe au dernier demi-siècle". In: *Actes du 16ème Congrès International des Linguistes, Paris, 1997*. Paris - Amsterdam - London: Elsevier. [CD-ROM]

1999

– "Der Wirkungsbereich des Wackernagelschen Gesetzes und die Entstehung der Präpositionen". In: P. ANREITER *et al.* (eds.), *Studia Celtica et Indogermanica. Festschrift für Wolfgang Meid zum 70. Geburtstag*, 385-396. Budapest: Archaeolingua Alapítvány.
– "On the Nature and Essence of Laryngeal Reflexes With Glimpses on the Emergence of a Terminological Usage". *Historische Sprachforschung* 112. 175-187.

2000

– "A Tentative Indo-European Reconstruction of Some Latin Pronominal Functions". In: G. CALBOLI (ed.), *Papers on Grammar V*, 1-14. Bologna: CLUEB.

2001

– ***Un demi-siècle de linguistique européenne***. (= *Mémoires de la Société de Linguistique de Paris*, n.s. 10). Paris - Leuven: Peeters.

– "La conception de la diction épique dans l'esprit des poètes républicains et leurs successeurs". In: Cl. MOUSSY *et al.* (eds.), *De lingua Latina novae quaestiones. Actes du Xe Colloque International de Linguistique latine, Paris-Sèvres, 19-23 avril 1999*, 981-993. Leuven - Paris - Sterling: Peeters.

2003

– "Remarques à propos du genre grammatical en hébreu biblique". In: J. LENTIN – A. LONNET (eds.), *Mélanges David Cohen. Études sur le langage, les langues, les dialectes, les littératures offertes par ses élèves, ses collègues, ses amis [...] à l'occasion de son quatre-vingtième anniversaire*, 581-594. Paris: Maisonneuve & Larose.

THE JERUSALEM SCHOOL OF LINGUISTICS AND THE PRAGUE SCHOOL

by

Haiim B. Rosén

The text printed here was edited and prepared for publication by Hannah Rosén (with slight revisions by Pierre Swiggers).

ABBREVIATIONS USED

CP	=	Hans Jacob POLOTSKY, *Collected Papers*. Jerusalem: Magnes Press, 1971.
EW I	=	Haiim B. ROSÉN, *East and West. Selected Writings*, vol. I. München: Fink, 1982.
EW II	=	Haiim B. ROSÉN, *East and West. Selected Writings*, vol. II. München: Fink, 1984.
EW III	=	Haiim B. ROSÉN, *East and West III. Selected Writings*, vol. III. München: Fink, 1994.
LSPr	=	Josef VACHEK, *The Linguistic School of Prague*. Bloomington - London: Indiana University Press, 1966.
PrSRL	=	Josef VACHEK (ed.), *A Prague School Reader in Linguistics*. Bloomington - London: Indiana University Press, 1964.

THE JERUSALEM SCHOOL OF LINGUISTICS AND THE PRAGUE SCHOOL*

by

Haiim B. ROSÉN

When we venture to speak about the "École de Jérusalem" in the spirit of a noted German publisher who invited me, shortly after the foundation of the *Societas Linguistica Europaea*, to participate in a series of *Eigenschilderungen* of the important contemporary schools, we must not conceal that our mentor, the late Hans Jacob Polotsky, always objected to the use of this term. Without success, since I kept to it persistently. His maxim was that we do not talk about our methods, that we should indeed do research into languages and their facts according to our own method or methodology, but need not make this explicit. "Tun Sie gleich das Richtige, aber reden Sie nicht davon!" was his motto.

So it was, in a way, left to his followers to describe the means by which we obtain our not at all negligible results. I feel that the term "École de Jérusalem" has the right to exist, nay, is essential and required in the history of our discipline, not because I wish to contend that the Jerusalemite linguists all adhere to the methodological premises and postulates of this school, just as Josef Vachek did not insist concerning the Prague School[1]: the trends and fashions of the '50s and '60s have left their mark on a number of Israeli colleagues and researchers, who are inclined to work with some degree of orthodoxy — *per se* deplorable — in the spirit of a very different outlook; there

---

* Written version of a talk given at a special session of the Societatis Linguisticae Europaeae Sodalicium Israëlense on May 10th 1995 at Ben Gurion University of the Negev (Be'er-Sheva); the talk was attended by, *inter alios*, members of the present-day Prague School.

[1] On the diversity within the general perspective see in particular *LSPr*, 15–39 (chapter "The general pattern of the Prague theory"), and J. VACHEK, "The heritage of the Prague School to modern linguistic research", in: *Praguiana. Some Basic and Less Known Aspects of the Prague Linguistic School* (Amsterdam 1983), 255–274 [first published in *Zeitschrift für Anglistik und Amerikanistik* 27 (1979), 52–61].

is however something specifically and peculiarly characteristic in the working and thinking of the majority of the Jerusalemite scholars of language science of my generation and our disciples; while inspired by preceding schools, mainly the Prague School, their ways do not coincide with those of any other great school. Theirs is also not altogether identical with the outlook of the Prague School, but rather has in many respects built on it, grown out of its seeds, and widened its scope, so as to enhance and diversify its potential. We consequently think that it is not by virtue of our distinct location that we rightly deserve the name of 'school' at the side of other schools in linguistic centers of our times, old and new, the Prague one, the Copenhagen one, the Parisian and Geneva one, the Amsterdam one, that of Yale or MIT.

We have been fortunate to be able to found a department of linguistics at the Hebrew University in 1953, much earlier than the same was done in many European institutions of higher learning. The Hebrew term used was felt as closer to *Sprachwissenschaft* than to what many a contemporary would wish to dub 'linguistics', and so was the approach envisaged by us. It had all begun with the instinctive, but nevertheless enlightening recognition of the paramount importance of the concept of relevance or pertinence, which we found confirmed by the perusal of Trubetzkoy's *Grundzüge*. Conducive thereto was our German-philology inspired occupation with ancient languages, languages transmitted in writing, which compelled us to ponder, which of the distinctions of graphic signifiers were in fact functional on the level of actual sound. That sort of question was especially significant in our particular cultural setting, because most vocalization and punctuation systems of the tradition of Hebrew, and amongst them the one which pointed the way towards revived Hebrew speech, are largely sub-phonemic, in sharp contrast, at that, to Arabic vocalized writing which is strictly phonemic. There reigned — and still does to some extent — a false notion that every written symbol constituted a functional unit of its own, to the degree of identifying every grapheme with the then newly conceived notion of a 'phoneme'[2]. So it is understandable

[2] See Sh. MORAG, *The Vocalization Systems of Arabic, Hebrew and Aramaic: Their Phonetic and Phonemic Principles* (The Hague 1962).

that our *Fragestellungen* in this respect immediately directed structural linguistics towards a tangible and painfully unhappy antagonism to traditional Hebraistics[3]. That discipline manifested, at least as concerns research of the classical language, a conspicuously low degree of participation in the ways of our school and in probing into questions of theory and methodology in general, which is, I think, the case in most countries concerning the scientific study of their national language. It has also to do with an intense dislike of the synchronistic attitude, and of the separation of the synchronic and diachronic viewpoints[4] in general, strengthened by reluctance, mainly on the part of religious scholars, to desecrate a sacred language and the study of its traditional texts by using methods considered modernist and smacking of heretics; thus it was the fate of our structuralist school to fall into, and to develop inside a not altogether favourable setting of policy and practice; the importance of an analogous circumstance was justly appreciated by Trnka in his description of the roots of the Prague School and the ideological structure of the period[5].

The reception of the concepts of relevance and neutralization as well as that of free variation provided the Jerusalem School with a working instrument of extreme importance, which characterized our work due to the fact that the terminology operative in it remained in our perspective a tool which — somewhat inclining towards Hjelmslevian thinking — was not aimed at, nor in its application limited to one single level of analysis, but rather consistently employed, unlike Praguian practice, on all conceivable levels[6], and also from the paradigmatic as well as

---

[3] As reflected, e.g., in Z. BEN-ḤAYYIM, *An Ancient Language in a New Reality* (*Lešonénu La'am* 35–37) [Hebrew; repr. 1992 in *The Struggle for a Language* (Jerusalem), 37–85]. Cf. now the chapter "The debate over the normalcy of Hebrew" in R. KUZAR, *Hebrew and Zionism* (Berlin - New York 2001), 137–196.

[4] Cf. *LSPr*, 16, on the lack of appreciation on the part of the Neogrammarians and their followers for any synchronistic research.

[5] In a lecture delivered at the Czech Academy in 1943; translated as an appendix in *LSPr*, 152–165. Cf. however the propitious atmosphere, as described in *LSPr*, 15–20, into which the *Cercle Linguistique de Prague* first stepped.

[6] VACHEK (in *LSPr*) deplored the relative lack of interest members of the Prague Circle took in extra-phonological analysis: "Specific Prague contributions to morphological problems were [and still are! H.R.] much less numerous than concrete contributions dealing with phonological problems" (p. 82).

from the syntagmatic angle; in this last respect our practice tallies with Prague School ways, as described in Trnka's exposition of its structural method[7]. Inversely, it would appear that the application of Prague-type paradigmatic tools of analysis when dealing with features of syntagmatics somehow characteristically sets our school apart from a number of other types of European structuralisms or 'functionalisms'.

The dichotomy *langue/parole* is, of course, fundamental to our work, but is on no account to be interpreted in the sense of a performance arising out of a statable competence, which in our view cannot be grasped by scientific means. From an angle of *Wissenschaftsgeschichte*, we are very much interested in the development of the notion of *parole* vs. *langue*, or *Rede* vs. *Sprache*, which triggered, also from the historical point of view, our interest in Humboldt, whom we have recognized to have applied this dichotomy in conjunction with numerous other concepts and whose ways and views we have therefore been studying rather intensively in the past decade or so. He can only by a very distorted view be considered as belonging to, or being a forerunner of, any linguistic persuasion other than structuralism[8].

Naturally, our work commences with the materialization in *parole*, i.e. from what is with some condescension called the 'surface'; this being the only set of phenomena which can be objectively seized and therefore constituting our 'datum' at all levels is at the same time a guard against unbridled universalism. From here derives what should be considered the axiom of our working procedure: Two different forms of expression must be considered as being of different function, as long as the contrary is not proven. This entails a twofold consequence: first that it is incumbent on us to discover the exact nature of this difference of function; and secondly that the *onus probandi* rests on whoever contends that they are not functionally different, i.e. either

---

[7] B. TRNKA *et al.*, "Prague structural linguistics", *Philologica Pragensia* 1 (1958), 33–40 = *PrSRL*, 468–480, at p. 475f.

[8] See my "Wilhelm von Humboldt – philosopher or the first structural linguist?", *Bulletin of the Language Institute of Gakushuín University* 12 (1989), 3–39 = *EW* III, 37–73. Cf. Vachek's account (*LSPr*, 16f.) of the way Mathesius blended Humboldt's approach with that of the Neogrammarians.

alternating according to a statable conditioning factor or in true free variation, that is, not even belonging to different modes or styles of expression — since the impact of 'function' in our eyes is not limited to content. This fundamental attitude and conception of our scholarly duty has brought about some of the most significant findings of *faits de langue*, which have introduced important new distinctions and identifications of features of the individual languages in the research of which we have been engaging.

For the correct evaluation of the Praguian Jerusalem School at its beginning it is important to remember that Polotsky underlined in his teaching that in the study of ancient language forms we have to rise above the servile thinking which leads to establishing and reproducing phonic realities; of interest are only the functional relations inside the sound system, as they are reflected in writing.

This attitude is all the more important since traditionalists and purists in language education in revived Hebrew advocated — as a token of faithfulness to the language of our forefathers — the imitation of some vague, and largely unsubstantiated so-called 'Semitic', i.e. Arabocentric, restitution of Biblical Hebrew sounds according to consonantal and vocalic graphemes. Polotsky, in two very early articles of his, "Zur koptischen Lautlehre" (1931, 1933)[9], at the very onset — long before the *Grundzüge* — of attempts to define the phoneme notion, described the phonological essence of certain Coptic orthographic habits and was successful in showing that certain differences observed between the Coptic dialects involved, in fact, orthographic usage rather than pertinent reality in the language. He discovered the existence of nasal and other sonants in that language, and established the environments in which certain consonantic materializations occurred. I may add here the publication, in 1962, of a phonological and morphological description of the language of a Classical Greek author[10], in whose phonological section the totality of Praguian techniques was used along with

[9] I–II: *Zeitschrift für ägyptische Sprache und Altertumskunde* 67 (1931), 74–77; 69 (1933), 125–129 = *CP*, 348–351; 358–362.

[10] My *Laut- und Formenlehre der herodotischen Sprachform* (Heidelberg 1962).

its terminology. This work was hailed as the first structural analysis of a language form published in Germany, even entailing here and there the creation of new German terminology. Ironically, but understandably, some reviews from the pen of Classical philologists expressed uneasiness about this phonological analysis, evidently incomprehensible to them. I think that nevertheless by this book we have exerted a certain influence on a segment of European philological discipline.

Thus it became part and parcel of our basic working habits to acknowledge that in the treatment of ancient languages one cannot start from assumed physical realities, and that the only realities which we are able to seize are phonological rather than phonetic ones. On the other hand, this attitude was conducive to cornering phonetics into a somewhat marginal position comparable to the position of phonetics in the Prague School, which considered phonology and phonetics as separate sciences[11]; finally the teaching of phonetics proper was established outside our department, principally in the framework of research into the manifold liturgical Hebrew tradition of reading in the Jewish communities[12]. On the other hand this attitude strengthened distributional tendencies which — according to all indications — were not fully present in the Prague School, at least in its original shape, and are highly characteristic of our philological procedures, by which we strive to uncover the facts of structure, linguistic as well as textual. Not unlike directing phonetics to a separate area of occupation, we deem the study of stylistics and language styles, that is, individual authors' styles, as being principally part of the aesthetic and historical aspects of the discipline of literature.

One of the important applications of this distributional approach was the view that different types of communication constitute different textual environments, in which distinctive oppositions function differently. By environments, I am

---

[11] As propounded by Trnka and Vachek (*LSPr*, 42f.), noting however that "their mutual relation is certainly much more complex than the radical line drawn in the early thirties was likely to reveal".

[12] See now Sh. MORAG, "The project of the language traditions of Israeli communities: Jewish languages – collection and research" [Hebrew], in *Papers on Jewish Languages* (Jerusalem 1987, ed. M. Ben-Asher), 153–161.

specifically referring to segments representing Benveniste's[13] and Weinrich's[14] *'récit historique'* and *'Erzählen'* vs. *'discours'* and *'Besprechen'*, respectively, and the like. The importance of the original Jerusalemite contribution in this respect was the application of this type of distinction to the Classical languages, more exactly to their employ of verbal tenses: for Latin by Hannah Rosén in a now frequently referred to analysis of Plinius' letters[15] and for Greek in an (unpublished) doctoral dissertation by Sarah Meron on Lysias' forensic orations[16]. The theoretical innovation here is that we improve on the dictum that functional *differentiae specificae* be established through examination of the occurrences of two or more contrasting items, by requiring them to be examined separately for any environment in which these oppositions are not neutralized (while maintaining a *Gesamtbedeutung*); to wit, a distinction between, say, a Latin imperfect and a narrative perfect has disparate functions in a framework of *'récit'* and in that of *'discours'*.

In our outlook, which in the empirical side of its research enlarged the scope of validity of the analytical conceptions of the Prague School to all levels of analysis, there was one fact of Praguian phonology to which we attached particular attention, that of boundary signals. Recognizing that these signals were indications of segmentation, *démarcation*, rather than of sutures, we were obliged to point to the inappropriateness of the American-born term of 'juncture'. Eventually we were able to show that in every segment there was a complexity of types of boundaries, according to the status of the element at either side of the boundary: the signals are constituted by phonological entities for the purpose of morphological segmentation, and by morphological entities for the purpose of syntactic segmentation. In recognizing the multifariousness of boundary types, e.g. a

---

[13] "Les relations de temps dans le verbe français", *BSL* 54/1 (1959), 69–82 = *Problèmes de linguistique générale* I (Paris 1966), 237–250.

[14] *Tempus. Besprochene und erzählte Welt* (Stuttgart 1964).

[15] "'Exposition und Mitteilung' – The imperfect as a thematic tense-form in the letters of Pliny", in Hannah and Haiim B. Rosén, *On Moods and Tenses of the Latin Verb* (München 1980), 27–48.

[16] *The Conception of Time and its Progress and their Expression in the Verbal System of the Greek of Lysias* [Hebrew University dissertation 1988].

boundary signal between a radical base and a stem-forming affix, one between a stem and an inflectional ending, etc.[17], we were inspired by a very similar line of thought maintained by the ancient Indian grammarians in their quest for criteria for the various types of sandhi, whose importance was underlined by Wilhelm von Humboldt (in: *Über die Verschiedenheit des menschlichen Sprachbaues* [ed. Buschmann], p. 140) as the determining factor in establishing formal indications of the *Einheit des Wortes*, so fundamental in his doctrine. Recognizing the paramount importance of the boundary signals and their identification by the message receiver who would be unable to 'understand' a spoken message without their identification (just like an Indian reader in *scriptio continua* in ancient times), we not only put to use this notion of boundary signals in order to help in providing a means of defining a 'word' (in the sense of *mot phonétique*) other than impressionistically by its content or autonomy of sense, but also elucidated a number of otherwise puzzling features in the framework of the Classical Hebrew systems of punctuation and vocalization, such as the 'dageš euphonicum' and pausal vs. contextual forms.

Contrary to the ill-named American doctrine claiming the existence of two or at the most three 'junctures', it is — to the best of my knowledge — only the Prague and the Jerusalem Schools which have integrated the doctrine of boundary signals into the complete description of language systems. We feel that in addition to its application to individual languages it might still be developed into a rigorous procedure of the still very deficient syntactic segmentation of complex sentences in mechanical analysis and translation of texts.

The doctrine of phonological *Grenzsignale* plays a very important role in the separation of foreign elements and proper nouns from the basic native or inherited stock of vocabulary. Just to recall Trubetzkoy's example, a sequence [pts] is in contemporary German either a boundary signal or an indication of a proper name such as *Leipzig*. Retrospectively we can state

[17] See my "An outline of a general theory of juncture", in *Studies in Egyptology and Linguistics in Honour of H.J. Polotsky* (Jerusalem 1964), 153–189 = *EW* I, 19–55, also for the application of the theory to Sanskrit, Attic Greek, and Biblical Hebrew.

that such insights inspired all of our phonemic analysis of Israeli Hebrew, a language which is very rich in non-naturalized loans and whose inventory of (mainly personal) names of non-native origin and structure is exceptionally large. In 1950, an American printer and semi-amateur linguist, Ralph W. Weiman, published a mimeographed monograph, ostensibly directed at distinguishing foreign elements from native ones in Modern Hebrew[18]; this objective led him to establish a complete Prague-type and Prague-developed phonemic system, including accentuation features, of contemporary Hebrew; in that way he could identify any lexeme or form deviating from the rules of that system as in fact foreign[19]. Weiman's findings are at the basis of the structure I posited in the first synchronic description of Israeli Hebrew in 1955[20], and which I feel has not lost its validity up to this day. At that time, of course, we were already at a period in which other outlooks had revealed themselves and are recognizable as forerunners of research in the generativist school: while, for instance, not recognizing the extra-systemicity of foreign elements and proper names, linguists of a different conviction hold that every phonic materialization current in language use must be given systemic status. Thus while for us there is, e.g., a single chuintant phoneme in Israeli Hebrew, materialized as either unvoiced [š], *terme marqué*, or voiced [ž] in assimilatory positions; or a single mid-front vowel /e/, realized according to certain conditions as either closed [ẹ] or open [ɛ], those scholars, amongst them the late Haim Blanc, maintained that the isolated, albeit current, existence of words like *žakɛt* would vouch for the introduction of two more phonemes in our phonemic grid.

At this point it may be appropriate to show to what degree the recognition of the notion of systemicity or the wholeness and coherence in a language system and of the relation rather than

[18] With the consequently unrevealing title *Native and Foreign Elements in a Language: A Study in General Linguistics Applied to Modern Hebrew* (Philadelphia 1950).

[19] This is strongly reminiscent of the impact the recognition of foreign influences and bilingualism had on the initial stages of the Prague School (*LSPr*, 25f.).

[20] *Ha'ivrit Šelanu* [*Our Hebrew Language*] (Tel Aviv 1955), 138–245, followed in 1958 for the syntactic level by *'Ivrit Tova* [*Good Hebrew*] (Jerusalem).

the item as the only true linguistic element or feature is a notion which has pervaded the ways of thought and work of Jerusalemite scholars.

Again, we point to the late *Altmeister* Polotsky as the inspiration of such ways of thought. Dealing with certain composite tense forms, that went, failing a more intelligent term, by the name of 'second' tenses and were taken, due to their equal translatability to that of the so-called 'first' tenses, to be just some insignificant variants thereof, he inquired not into what they meant, so to speak, but into what the difference was between their function and the function of the non-composite first tenses. His answer of 1944[21] lay, surprisingly enough, on the level of the communicative function (to which we shall come later), with these tenses revealed as being marked for non-rhematicity. Thereby Polotsky revolutionized Coptic syntax and Classical Egyptian morphology[22]. Trying to emulate him, we were induced to handle in an analogous manner[23] similar elements of Greek morphosyntax, the ἦν διδάσκων (literally "he was teaching") type, which had mystified quite a few generations of Greek scholars: while no function was ascribed to them in Classical Greek, they were used intensively in certain theologically important Neotestamentarian passages. In this work we were obliged to attach paramount significance to another concept of Praguian analysis, that of neutralization, with an archi-element, which more often than not physically coincides with one of the elements constituting a distinctive opposition. Needless to say, many a school outside the Prague tradition rejects with contempt this notion as though "once a phoneme" were "always a phoneme", or rather a morpheme in our case. But the problem of the form at issue could not be solved without having recourse to the concept of neutralization, since with certain morphophonemically definable classes of verbs or verb forms, periphrastic forms must — as every beginning student of Greek knows —

[21] *Études de syntaxe copte* (Le Caire 1944), 20–98 = *CP*, 125–202.

[22] "The 'emphatic' sdm.n.f. form", *Revue d'égyptologie* 11 (1957), 109–117; "Ägyptische Verbalformen und ihre Vokalisation", *Orientalia* 33 (1964), 267–285 = *CP*, 43–70.

[23] "Die 'zweiten' Tempora des Griechischen. Zum Prädikatsausdruck beim griechischen Verbum", *Museum Helveticum* 14 (1957), 133–154 = *EW* I, 303–324.

replace monolectic ones, thereby neutralizing the distinguishing formal feature. The verb classes concerned, by the way, are not the same at every period of the history of Greek, which for us again underlined the importance of considering diachrony as a sequence of synchronies[24]. So we isolated the cases of neutralization and archi-elements first, in order to be able to effectively examine the functions of the forms under scrutiny in conditions of genuine opposition and selectability. We may state with quite some satisfaction that this procedure, the preliminary isolation of neutralization environments prior to engaging in any attempt at uncovering functions, and especially on the levels superior to phonology, has become standard procedure in our school, and one will hardly find here any study of real significance, in which this methodological requirement has not been taken care of.

In the case under discussion the result was, again, the discovery of a non-rhematic function of the Greek periphrastic tenses, provided these are selectable rather than environmentally conditioned. Generally speaking, it is precisely this strict and typically Praguian procedure which brought forth the most substantial advances in grammatical analysis of which the Jerusalem School can boast: principally in the area of the syntax of nominal phrases, the distinctiveness was uncovered of the genitival and the adjectival adnominal constructions in Latin by Hannah Rosén[25], after carefully eliminating the areas of neutralization and thereby conclusively breaking with the somehow Slav-inspired notion of Wackernagel that "fatherly love" and "love of father" were, so to speak, 'the same'[26]; something similar was obtained, by operating with genuinely contrastive positions, for the Greek of Homer[27]; for Hebrew, on the other hand, we had

---

[24] "Les successivités", in *Mélanges Marcel Cohen* (The Hague - Paris 1970), 113–129 = *EW* I, 56–72.

[25] *Studies in the Syntax of the Verbal Noun in Early Latin* (München 1981).

[26] J. WACKERNAGEL, "Genitiv und Adjektiv", in *Mélanges Saussure* (Paris 1908), 125–152, esp. 137ff. = J.W., *Kleine Schriften* (Göttingen 1953), 1346–1373, esp. 1358ff. = *Vorlesungen über Syntax* II (Basel ²1928), 68–72; Wackernagel's presentation had already been contested by Einar LÖFSTEDT, who introduced semantic distinctions between the two in his own "Genetiv und Adjektiv" chapter of *Syntactica* I (Lund ²1942), 106-124.

[27] In the chapter "Ablativ und Adjektiv" of my *Strukturalgrammatische Beiträge zum Verständnis Homers* (Amsterdam ¹1967, München ²1984), 85–112,

concentrated on dissipating, by means of the very same procedure of analysis and after some heated discussion, the false notion of the equivalence between the direct and bare connection of two nouns in one nominal phrase, the so-called construct state, and their junction through a prepositional link of the type of "of"[28], thus distinguishing the type "my aunt's murder" from the one of "the murder of my aunt". Here we could also bring to light the existence, in Israeli Hebrew, of a distinction between inalienable and alienable possession, which would keep, *inter alia*, "Cohen's book", *terme marqué*, distinct from "the book of Cohen". We have lately seen similar results obtained by the same procedure for Slavic and Baltic languages by Lea Sawicki[29], who, on examining means of expression for this distinction on all levels and putting the emphasis on problems of case-syntax, subdivided the dative in its relation to other cases according to its being or not what is termed 'sympathetic', i.e., related or not to inalienability, or appurtenance. Inalienability or, respectively, non-inalienability, was found to be marked by a variety of distinctions, morphologically in Coptic and Israeli Hebrew, syntactically in Chinese, in Indo-European in general and Baltic specifically, lexically in some other languages.

We have made reference in this context to the term of markedness, duly distinguishing in our thought 'marking' on the formal level, i.e., conceiving of a term as *merkmaltragend* (or *merkmalhaft*, *-haltig*), and markedness on the content or functional level. On grounds of this very important difference, expressed in Russian by the pair of terms *priznakovyj – markirovannyj*[30], we attribute markedness or distinct characterization

---

in critique of Paul NEUMANN, *Das Verhältnis des Genitivs zum Adjektiv im Griechischen* (Diss. Münster 1910), who did not proceed either synchronically or structurally.

[28] "Sur quelques catégories à expression adnominale en hébreu israélien", *BSL* 53/1 (1957/8), 316–344 = *EW* II, 41–69, and the chapter "New meanings: Attributes" ([1]1958, 116–179; [3]1977, 127–193) in *'Ivrit Tova* (above, note 20).

[29] "Expressions of inalienability in Polish", *Wiener Slawistischer Almanach* 29 (1992), 261–267; "Expressions of inalienability in Modern Lithuanian", *Linguistica Baltica* 5/6 (1997), 37–43.

[30] Tamás Gamkrelidze, orally. Cf. now Michel VIEL, *La notion de «marque» chez Trubetzkoy et Jakobson* (Lille - Paris 1984), 94–96, 676, on the vicissitudes of the two terms.

to one of the terms of an opposition, whether it has an overt mark or not. While Vachek acknowledges the discrepancy between the two for morphological correlation only[31], we think this conception should be taken account of, in order to avoid erroneous and misconceived results, on all levels of analysis. And when Roman Jakobson says[32] that "normally the markless (*merkmallosen*) forms are applied at the expense of the corresponding marked (*merkmalhaltigen*) forms" and explains it by the fact that the markless form functions in the linguistic conscience as a representative of both members of the correlative pair, he is — with all due respect — amalgamating the two concepts.

As for the verbal domain, I have always felt that the study of Greek voice could be much advanced by examining the functions of different voices in opposition, of the middle voice, for example, where it contrasts with either the active or the passive, and not where the opposition of voice is neutralized either in certain aspect stems or in specific lexematic entities; this approach led to — what is of more importance in our own cultural setting — doing away with utterly outdated notions about the so-called 'meanings' of the Hebrew conjugation stems, the so-called *binyanim*, about which much abuse was still current until very recently due to neglect of the concept of distinctive oppositions. Recent results were conducive to defining the different affixal verb stem formations, hitherto quasi-semantically described as causative, inchoative, privative, reflexive, redefining them (where in opposition to each other) as having contrasting valency[33]. It may even be that notably in Hebrew these verb forms acquire their meaning by virtue of the forms in which a given verb stem is apt to be used, due to the omnipresence of the inventory of potential uses in the minds of the speaker and

---

[31] In *LSPr*, 84f.

[32] In "Zur Struktur des russischen Verbums", in *Charisteria Guilelmo Mathesio oblata* (Praha 1932), 74–84 = *Selected Writings* II (The Hague 1972), 3–15 = *Form und Sinn* (München 1974), 55–67 at p. 64 = *PrSRL*, 347–359, at p. 357.

[33] Summed up in the sections "Valence" and "Extrasystemic (surviving) distinctions, lexicalizations", of my *Contemporary Hebrew* (The Hague - Paris 1977), 200-205.

hearer. From here dependency grammar, primarily based on contrasting valencies of lexemes that belong to one and the same verbal root, gained ground in this country considerably more than at many other centers of learning, as may be seen from the widely known studies which stem from here and are devoted to valency studies of, amongst others, French[34], Latin[35], Polish[36], all perfectly faithful to the methodological requirements that eventually became crystallized in our midst. We ascribe these achievements to our adherence to the requirements of the Prague School, in our particular shading thereof, because — as it would seem — some other schools, one at least, in proceeding deductively would lead aprioristically from ethnocentrically conceived 'meanings' to the generation of surface-forms, thereby depriving us of the possibility to genuinely understand language-specifically the functional essence of these language forms in the process of verbal communication.

It goes without saying that the tools of Prague-type analysis eventually bring about the correct establishment of grammatical categories by appropriately ordering and dividing the inventory of inflectional and periphrastic forms, examining their mutual exclusivity or, respectively, their compatibility; here we have adopted, of course, Trubetzkoy's strategy in establishing phoneme categories. We are thus in a position to establish a strictly language-specific inventory of existing categories, which is the principal barrier warding off falsifying and disturbing universalisms of any sort, with the notion of anisomorphism of languages serving as our constant guideline. For Hebrew we obtained a most important category which had not been recognized before, that of case, by distinguishing the substitutable uses of some nominal prefixes from the non-substitutable ones, in other words, by separating their neutralization positions from positions of pertinence and laying the groundwork for the notion of

---

[34] Mira ROTHENBERG, *Les verbes à la fois transitifs et intransitifs en français contemporain* (The Hague 1974).

[35] Review article by Hannah ROSÉN, with *prises de position* relative to the point at issue here, of H. HAPP, *Grundfragen einer Dependenz-Grammatik des Lateinischen* (*BSL* 73/2 [1978], 71–78).

[36] Lea SAWICKI, *Verb-Valency in Contemporary Polish* (Tübingen 1988).

case government[37], utterly independent of the semantics of the governing lexeme; rather, we were able to show these very properties of content as dependent upon the syntactic behaviour of the verbal lexeme in each and every instance. It must be borne in mind that after the prehistoric loss of final inflection in Hebrew, nothing remained that was comparable to the vulgarized and Latinocentric notion of 'case' which linked that concept to nominal inflection by endings. But we recognized those same functions in the inseparable prenominal morphemes that had been commonly termed *Verhältniswörter*. It may be noteworthy that this way of viewing things (which in the long run influenced even the teaching of syntactic analysis in Israeli secondary schools due to its capacity to refine dependency-grammatical distinctions) corresponded to an analogous discovery made concerning German, by Renate Steinitz[38], who in 1969 demonstrated that 'Objekte' may have the shape not only of inflected case-forms but also of prepositional phrases, thereby introducing, I think, the notion of *Präpositionalobjekt*, highly important for the development of dependency grammar in German-speaking countries and in the East-Berlin type of grammar of the *Gegenwartssprache* prior to its final takeover by adepts of the generative school.

Turning now to other areas of linguistic analysis, I should stress the great advance achieved by the minimal-pair technique in the area of lexical semantics. For a considerable period, Yishai Tobin (of whom, however, we cannot boast as a descendent of the Jerusalem School, being a representative of the so-called form–content analysis of the Columbia School) was able to 'excavate', so to speak, interesting sememes, mainly in the verbal area, by opposing, within their textual environments, suitable minimal pairs of English lexemes, such as *speak* vs. *talk* or *must* vs. *have to*, thereby underlining the usefulness of a Prague-type study of means of expression as compared to what I would describe as a much less promising though overused lexicographical technique: this technique obtains along the textual,

[37] The chapter "Superstitions: Objects and descriptions" of *'Ivrit Tova* (above, note 20), [1]85–112, [3]97–124.

[38] *Adverbial-Syntax* (Berlin 1969).

parole-bound occurrences of one single 'word' an impressionistic idea of what is common to all of them, trying to arrive at a meaning out of a sometimes fortuitous collection of references.

Let me recall at this juncture a dictum of Roman Jakobson's in response to a remark I made at the IXth Congress of Linguists in 1962, namely that for him the relationship between the different semantic uses, or references, and the meaning of a word was precisely the same as the one between allophones and a phoneme[39], a viewpoint which of course eliminates any idea of polysemy. While in the research of Hebrew lexical semantics, mainly that of the Biblical language, the other strategy, that of putting together attestations of one single word, had been applied for a long time almost exclusively, it was recently superseded by Prague-type semantic analyses of Biblical lexical entities by way of opposing contentwise similar words; this method has, however, not been carried much further for Hebrew, due to the untimely death of its principal promoter and representative, the late Eliezer Rubinstein[40].

We now can turn to syntax. Concerning syntax, the working methods of the Prague School (and its close relative, the Jerusalem School) are all the more important, as syntactic enquiry is the chief concern of the school that is its principal competitor (viz. the generativist school) but has at its disadvantage the fact that after discarding morphology and bypassing the notion of the phoneme[41], it uses entirely different procedures for each level or area of analysis, while we aspire — as I said at the beginning — to use a single fundamental technique of analysis to serve us at any level or area in which we might become interested.

Essentially thanks to the above-mentioned findings obtained by Polotsky, the consideration of the communicative function (on the plane of *énonciation*) has become lock, stock and barrel

[39] *PICL* IX (The Hague 1964), p. 365.

[40] See now in particular the articles of the second and third section of his collected writings, *Syntax and Meaning* (Tel Aviv 1998) [Hebrew].

[41] See however *LSPr*, 81, on the "remarkable revival of interest in problems of morphonology", with which Vachek accredits, unjustifiedly to my mind, the generativist approach.

of all syntactic work of the Jerusalem School about any given language, by any of our scholars. Let me say, for the sake of historical truth, that Polotsky, who did not formulate an explicit doctrine of the two or three kinds of syntactic function, unfolded his findings in 1944, fully independently of the renowned dicta by Mathesius. While it may be said that the Praguian communicative-level approach had lesser influence on general linguistics before it was heralded in a language other than Czech, say, by Firbas, Polotsky's doctrine which centered around the true recognition of the nature of the cleft sentence, mainly in French and English (which also figure prominently in Mathesius' work)[42], exerted practically no influence outside Jerusalem, since it was concealed in a study exclusively aimed at students of Late Egyptian and Coptic, who did not at first receive it with due attention, because its general linguistic implications were beyond their horizon.

Since the number and nomenclature of the syntactic functions play a key role, we should add that Polotsky did not acknowledge the autonomy of the grammatical and the third, let us call it actantial, functions. The question centers here around the nature of that so-called 'subject' that is not the one termed 'logical', not the one on the informational level. I personally feel that this one should be split into two, not including within the actantial (or rather, as I would have it, the agentive) function that agent that was termed in earlier generations the 'psychological' one. I myself would reserve the term 'psychological subject' for what is neither a grammatical nor a logical subject (or *thema*) in structures of the type *mir ist kalt* or, to use Vachek's Czech example, *Je mi zima*[43]; these structures are syntactically calqued into Israeli Hebrew and play generally an active role in diachronic syntax, since in most Western Indo-European languages such constructions became replaced with agentive constructions: *Mir träumt*, *me thinks* yield to *Ich träume*, *I think*, respectively,

---

[42] Especially in his posthumous *Functional Analysis of Present-Day English on a General Linguistic Basis* (Praha 1961) [Czech]. Vachek's English paraphrases of Russian sentences (*LSPr*, 90f.) do not reflect the full picture, since clefting is exemplified there only by sentences with a declined relative, not by an 'abstract' conjunctional subordinate clause.

[43] *LSPr*, 92.

that is, a psychological subject is replaced by an agentive subject[44].

To a more significant point of divergence: many of us feel somewhat uneasy about the time-honoured term 'functional sentence perspective'. The notion of perspective implies too much of the 'spatial', or 'dimensional'. It is intrinsically linked to an idea of directionality, or linearity, as though this syntactic function had no other manifestation than the order of the sentence constituents, a formula that has given rise to the mistaken idea, that what is logically prior — subsequently termed 'topic' — must come before, and the comment-rhema, after. Again largely as an outcome of Polotsky's work which showed that rhematicity/non-rhematicity was expressed by the choice of items within verbal morphology, we feel obliged to keep logical function apart from its formal expression, to view also these two as a pair of the nature of *signifié* vs. *signifiant*, and to inquire what means a given language disposes of in order to express the difference between a rhematic and a non-rhematic part of the sentence[45]. It is only by this approach that we can free ourselves from the utterly non-structuralistic point of view that a function which pertains to a sentence cannot be expressed in any other way than syntactically, while paradigmatic means of expression, whether lexical items or formational and inflectional morphemes, cannot serve anything above the level of isolated items. It is a special merit of scholars of the Jerusalem School to have uncovered, in the wake of Polotsky's work, the great variety of means of expression, apart from constituent order, in the area of information structure: morphological, principally in verbal morphology, in Coptic, Greek (as we have

---

[44] See on the diachrony of such replacement in Latin my "*Vterum dolet* und Verwandtes", *Folia Linguistica* 4 (1969), 135–147 = *EW* I, 254–266, and on the typological characterization of constructions with a psychological subject within the pool of impersonal constructions in "On some types of so-called 'impersonality' and verbal valency in Indo-European", in *Rekonstruktion und relative Chronologie. Akten der VIII. Fachtagung der Indogermanischen Gesellschaft, Leiden 1987* (Innsbruck 1992), 383–390 at p. 384 = *EW* III, 188–195, at p. 189.

[45] This approach is expounded in my "Rhème et non-rhème: entités de langue. Pour une typologie des moyens d'expression formels", *BSL* 82/1 (1987), 135–162 = *EW* III, 113–140.

shown above) and also in Latin[46]; syntactic splitting other than regular clefting in Latin and Biblical Hebrew[47]; focusing particles in, *inter alia*, Latin and Japanese[48]; prosodic features in Coptic[49]; case-government and even lexical distinctions[50] in Biblical Hebrew. In each and every case, particular attention is placed, of course, on the identification of the *terme marqué* in the binary opposition of the rhematic vs. the non-rhematic. On occasion, this approach has led to some first attempts at imparting a more formal character to what is commonly called *Textgrammatik*, thus in studies of Israeli Hebrew[51] and Coptic[52] literature.

---

[46] By means of analytical vs. synthetic verbal forms (Hannah ROSÉN, *Studies in the Syntax of the Verbal Noun* [*o.c.*, note 25], 130–159).

[47] Constructions such as *accidit/euenit quod* to highlight attitudinal adverbs (Hannah ROSÉN, "General subordinators and sentence complements", in *Subordination and other Topics in Latin. Proceedings of the Third Colloquium on Latin Linguistics, Bologna 1985* [Amsterdam - Philadelphia 1989, ed. G. Calboli], 197–218); the *et/atque quidem* et sim. construction (Hannah ROSÉN, "La coordination asymétrique comme critère de fonction syntaxique en latin", *L'information grammaticale* 46 [1990], 34–37); see also note 46. Splitting within Hebrew nominal phrases that comprise quantifiers (numerals) is dealt with in my "Constituants pluricomponentiels et caractérisation de la fonction énonciative", in *La phrase: Énonciation et information*, *MSL* n.s. 2 (1994), 53–73, at p. 65.

[48] Just for example, on Latin *demum* "then", "at last" > "exclusively" (Hannah ROSÉN, "*demum*, a message-articulating particle", in *Florilegium Historiographiae Linguisticae* [Louvain-la-Neuve 1993], 173–184); on the intricate interplay of *ga* and *wa* in Japanese propositional structure (Kyoji TSUJITA in an [unpublished] Hebrew University seminar paper and in his *Textbook of Modern Japanese* [Jerusalem 1987]).

[49] H.J. POLOTSKY, "Zur koptischen Wortstellung", *Orientalia* 30 (1961), 294–313 = *CP*, 398–417.

[50] In the shape of the 1st person sg. pronoun (*'ăniy* non-predicative *terme marqué* vs. *'ånoχiy terme non marqué*): "אנכי et אני. Essai de grammaire, interprétation et traduction", in *Mélanges André Neher* (Paris 1975), 253–272 = *EW* II, 262–281.

[51] In various studies by Maya FRUCHTMAN, notably "Parataxis and hypotaxis as a criterion of the style of text types", *Balshanut 'Ivrit* 2 (1970), 29–45 [Hebrew]; *Literary Language: Style and Syntax in Hebrew Literature* (Tel Aviv 1990) [Hebrew].

[52] In the Sahidic dialect of Shenoute: Ariel SHISHA-HALEVY, *Coptic Grammatical Categories* (Roma 1986).

We put into practice our belief in a hierarchy of the needs, so to speak, of each plane of language: the availability of a tool, whether morphological, syntactic or lexical, for the structuration of the message is conditional on its being expendable on the grammatical plane. Such an established hierarchy is not universal, yet the priority of the message-structuring plane over the stylistic one, and of the grammatical plane over the message-structuring one is common to numerous genetically and typologically different languages[53].

Most of the researchers that adhere to our school proceed in sentential syntax according to a particular type of pattern syntax, which is their answer to the universalistic or unilinguistically based postulates of generative syntax: it introduces a number of sentence models, never exceeding the amount necessary, but is distinctly different from the universalistic view of considering all sentences of a language as derivational materializations of a single syntactic structure. This is achieved by describing the sentences as exhaustively as possible in terms of the parts of speech that occur in their pivotal structure.

To give only a few very simple examples:

1. A pattern consisting of a lexeme of existence + infinitive phrase has potential or necessitative meaning in post-Biblical Hebrew: *yeš laʿăsot maššehu* "Something has to be done".

2. A pattern of a first (more specific) noun and a second one as pivots has inherently possessive-categorizing meaning in Biblical Hebrew: *'ăniy tᵊfilåh* "I am a man of prayer", while an equally built pattern in Israeli Hebrew is equational (just like the pattern 'noun phrase plus adjective'): *hu' ba'aya* "He is a problem".

3. In Classical Greek, a pattern involving non-initially, i.e. as a copula, the verb of "being" may be equational or circumstantial; when it includes the same verb initially and is followed e.g. by an infinitive, it is an expression of potentiality, e.g. ἔστι ἰδεῖν "It may be seen".

Extremely lucid and historically instructive syntactic descriptions of this type were elaborated by Polotsky for Coptic[54] and

[53] As has been shown for modern German, Israeli Hebrew and Attic Greek ("Rhème et non-rhème" [*a.c.*, note 45], 152–156 = *EW* III, 130–134).

[54] Now in the two volumes of his *Grundlagen des koptischen Satzbaus* (Atlanta 1987-90, 2 vols.).

Neo-Syriac[55], for Classical Greek by Nimrod Barri[56], and for Biblical[57] as well as Israeli Hebrew[58] by myself, joining to them comparative glimpses on Indo-European and Semitic sentence patterns in general.

The way to recognizing the relation between the multiple sentence models as a relation between the different members of a paradigm was simple; now all features engrained in a paradigm, in particular that of the functionally different *valeur* of each of its members, were made effective for the members of this paradigm, to the extent of searching, wherever this was possible, for the *terme non marqué* of the — often non-binary — paradigmatic category. This could go as far as looking for, and discovering, the semantic difference between copulaless and copula-bearing nominal sentences (i.e. those with a nominal form as the predicative term), the copula being a pronominal entity, somewhat comparable, for example, to Russian *eto*. In these types of predication, rhematic orientation in verbless sentences is normally concomitant with prosodic degrading, i.e. enclisis of the copula. In Coptic, similarly to Biblical Hebrew, the tonic pronoun *pai* serves as a demonstrative rheme ("It is this, that such and such a thing is"), while its atone counterpart is not sentence-initial, and its shorter form *pe* characterizes the preceding noun as rhematic. The same is true of Biblical Hebrew *hu'*. Analogously, the 1st person sg. pronoun *'ånoχiy*, unlike its weaker counterpart *'ăniy*[59], must be taken as rhematic, e.g. in the first commandment: *'ånoχiy 'ădonay 'ĕloheyχa* etc. "It is me who is your God [who led thee out of Egypt, and [i.e. therefore] thou shalt not have other gods before me]". By the same token, using the lexical identity of certain pronominal copulas as an indication, it is possible to state that Israeli Hebrew, contrary to its Biblical ancestor, is one of the very rare languages — some

---

[55] "Neusyrische Konjugation", *Orientalia Suecana* 33–35 (1984–86), 323–332.

[56] *Clause-Models in Antiphontean Greek* (München 1977).

[57] "On some types of verbless sentences in Biblical Hebrew", in *Report of the 3rd World Congress for Jewish Studies, Jerusalem 1961* (Jerusalem 1965), 167–173 [Hebrew] = *EW* II, 221–228 [Hebrew].

[58] "Sentence Patterns", in the second edition of *'Ivrit Tova* (Jerusalem 1967), 197–302.

[59] See note 50.

scholars say the only one — in which analytic and synthetic predication (in the Kantian sense) as well as comment-making predication were distinguished by syntactic patterning. It is my impression that the notion of syntagmas being terms of a paradigm, while based on a distinctly Praguian procedure of analysis which considers forms of expression in their mutual opposition, is an important innovation of the Jerusalem School.

On these grounds the content of a sentence was viewed, as the examples above show, as a combination of the function of its pattern and the functions of every one of its constituents, lexematic ones as well as function words; we inquire not only what means of expression of any level — lexical, morphological or syntactical — are available to express rhematicity, or respectively, non-rhematicity, in the languages which we investigate, but also, in the event that the means of expression in question is a syntagmatic one, what order properties in fact underlie the message-articulating function, that is, whether the so-called topic in the basic neutral type of sentence really 'physically' precedes the rhema, or comment. That such is the case only in part of the languages is one of the important tenets of the Jerusalem School which we were compelled to recognize, thus breaking with the unjustifiedly universalistic notion of "topics coming first" or topicalization meaning nothing else than fronting, and conceiving a fresh approach, that of establishing the "rhematic orientation"[60], i.e. posing the question "When does a progressive movement of the sentence lead towards the rhematic element and when does the rhema come first in the sentence?", an orientation which we would term "regressive". This approach was almost forcibly inspired by the fact that a language whose syntax we now very intensively intend to study, namely Biblical Hebrew, is one in which that orientation is from the rhematic to the less rhematic; only thus the true purport of its sentences comes to light. This structure is evident in phrases built upon the ancient Semitic regressive model, such as Πλατεῖα ἡ πύλη καὶ εὐρύχωρος ἡ ὁδὸς ἡ ἀπάγουσα εἰς τὴν ἀπώλειαν, *Lata porta et spatiosa uia est quae ducit ad perditionem* (Matth. 7:13); when being absorbed by speech communities such as the modern

[60] See my "Constituants pluricomponentiels" (*a.c.*, note 47].

European ones and — *nota bene*! — Contemporary Hebrew in which a normal progressive rhematic orientation prevails, such sentences were easily recognized and classed as reflecting an elevated, highly rhetorical or sacred register; in Christian European speech communities this sentence pattern constitutes one of the Biblisms that enriched their stylistic inventory; in Israeli Hebrew it is felt as rhetoricizing.

The Prague-School-born notion of *Sprachbund*, of affinities acquired, has played a very important role in our linguistic activity, because — as I have already alluded to — it is not possible to state the position of Israeli Hebrew within the languages of civilization of our times without recourse to that concept: Israeli Hebrew is part of the European *Sprachbund*, and virtually all phenomena of convergence which take place in the languages of that community in our generation, have been emerging likewise in Israeli Hebrew, notably in the domains of word formation and syntax. It goes without saying that the acknowledgment of this fact has not been enthusiastically welcomed by purists or traditionalists, because these developments come at the expense of typically Semitic features. But it must also be taken into account that Hebrew is the only Semitic language which takes part in that *Sprachbund*; I would have added 'typologically', were it not for the fact that some of us do operate with a notion of typology, to a large degree developed in our midst, that is not congruent with that of the founders of the *Sprachbund* concept, but much closer to the notion of *Sprachtypen* established by Wilhelm von Humboldt.

While the members of the Jerusalem School are profoundly convinced that the Prague School methods as applied by us are the most expedient tools for advancing research methods and achieving the genuine goals of language science, they are at the same time fully aware of the fact that this cannot and should not apply to the boundary sciences. For some of these, Prague-type analysis is of very little use, and occasionally a rather generative-type approach is here the most promising. But for one of the more important outbranchings of language science, that is for language didactics, mainly in the realm of teaching foreign languages, the structural-functional approach, clad in contrastive analysis, is still the one most successfully applied. In our occupation with literary texts, principally ancient ones, it is felt that since the comprehension of the original hearer or reader of those literary works is of course based on the language of the time, it is precisely and uniquely the functional analysis of the structure of that language that brings us closer to creating a way of understanding these texts the way an ancient audience or readership did. Understanding, not interpreting, since interpretation is not part of the direct comprehension of texts by the ancient audience. This should be well borne in mind not only by students of literatures of remote periods and not only by students of ancient theoretical works, but — in our cultural set-up — first and foremost by philologists of the Scriptures. No presupposed sense of what the Book says must enter and falsify our deliberation of the linguistic meaning. It is also from here that the attitude of the "Jerusalem Praguians" towards what is currently termed *Textlinguistik* can be understood. As long as the study of a literary text deals with the means of expression in language, as long as it studies the compatibility or incompatibility of means of expression co-occurring with one another in the same text, this still constitutes *Textgrammatik* and can be regarded as being inside the limits of our discipline, whose aim is the uncovering of truths about language. But as soon as it settles solely for the *contenu* of what is said or written and the relation of elements of that *contenu*, narrative or otherwise, to each other, it is outside it; it may then belong to literary science. I would not take it upon myself to judge whether it truly is or not. However, this is where I and many of my colleagues stand in this respect.

Let me add in conclusion of this brief outline of points of contact and divergence between the two schools that, just like the typical Praguians, we too apply the structuralist method to diachronic studies in which we engage, no less than to synchronic ones, and that we too can pride ourselves on having kept an open mind and on striving to remain undogmatic, having never formed — to borrow Vachek's words[61] — a dogmatically closed body, while united in the basic acceptance of the structuralist and functionalist standpoint, or, in Jakobson's

[61] *LSPr*, 66.

formulation of 1963[62], aiming towards a *means–ends* model of language.

It is by virtue of most of the aspects I have put in center stage in my *raisonnement*, that we shall be able to preserve the essence and nature of linguistics, *Sprachwissenschaft*, as a science dealing with human language, and indeed as the only science which deals with it, human language being the only object which our discipline is meant to treat and scrutinize.

[62] R. JAKOBSON, "Efforts towards a means–ends model of language in interwar continental linguistics", in *Trends in Modern Linguistics 1930–1960* (Utrecht 1963, ed. by Chr. MOHRMANN *et al.*), 104–108 [repr. in *PrSRL,* 481–485].

TABLE OF CONTENTS

PRINTED ON PERMANENT PAPER • IMPRIME SUR PAPIER PERMANENT • GEDRUKT OP DUURZAAM PAPIER - ISO 9706
N.V. PEETERS S.A., WAROTSTRAAT 50, B-3020 HERENT